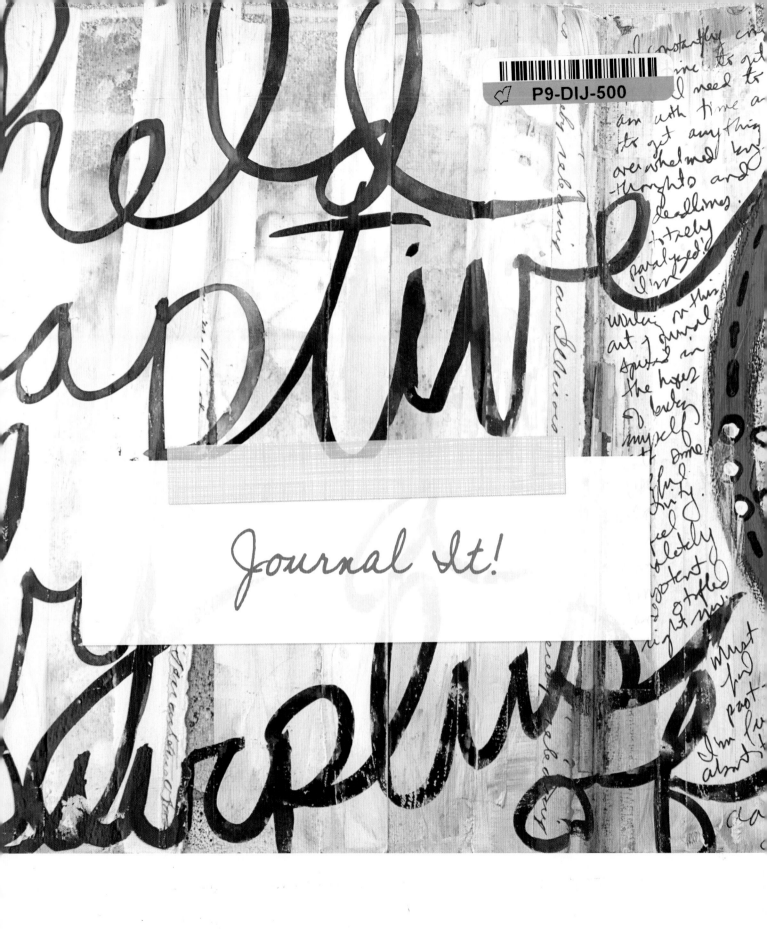

Journal It!

dreams

impulse

intuition

Journal It!

Perspectives in Creative Journaling

Jenny Doh

LARK CRAFTS

Asheville

LARK CRAFTS

An Imprint of Sterling Publishing
387 Park Avenue South
New York, NY 10016

If you have questions or comments about
this book, please visit: larkcrafts.com.

Doh, Jenny.
  Journal it! : perspectives in creative journaling / Jenny Doh. -- 1st ed.
       p. cm.
  Includes index.
  ISBN 978-1-4547-0355-6
  1. Artists' books. 2. Scrapbook journaling. 3. Artists' books. I. Title.
  TR501.D64 2012
  745.593'8--dc23
                              2012007050
10 9 8 7 6 5 4 3 2 1

First Edition

Published by Lark Crafts
An Imprint of Sterling Publishing Co., Inc.
387 Park Avenue South, New York, NY 10016

Text © 2012, Jenny Doh
Photography © 2012, Lark Crafts, an Imprint of Sterling Publishing Co., Inc., unless
otherwise specified

Distributed in Canada by Sterling Publishing,
c/o Canadian Manda Group, 165 Dufferin Street
Toronto, Ontario, Canada M6K 3H6

Distributed in the United Kingdom by GMC Distribution Services,
Castle Place, 166 High Street, Lewes, East Sussex, England BN7 1XU

Distributed in Australia by Capricorn Link (Australia) Pty. Ltd.,
P.O. Box 704, Windsor, NSW 2756 Australia

ISBN 13: 978-1-4547-0355-6

For information about custom editions, special sales, and premium and corporate
purchases, please contact Sterling Special Sales Department at 800-805-5489 or
specialsales@sterlingpub.com.

For information about desk and examination copies available to college and
university professors, requests must be submitted to academic@larkbooks.com.
Our complete policy can be found at www.larkcrafts.com.

Editor Linda Kopp

Art Director Kristi Pfeffer

Designer Raquel Joya

Photographer Cynthia Shaffer

Cover Designer Kristi Pfeffer

Copy Editors Nancy D. Wood,
Amanda Crabtree, Jana Holstein,
Sarah Meehan, Monica Mouet

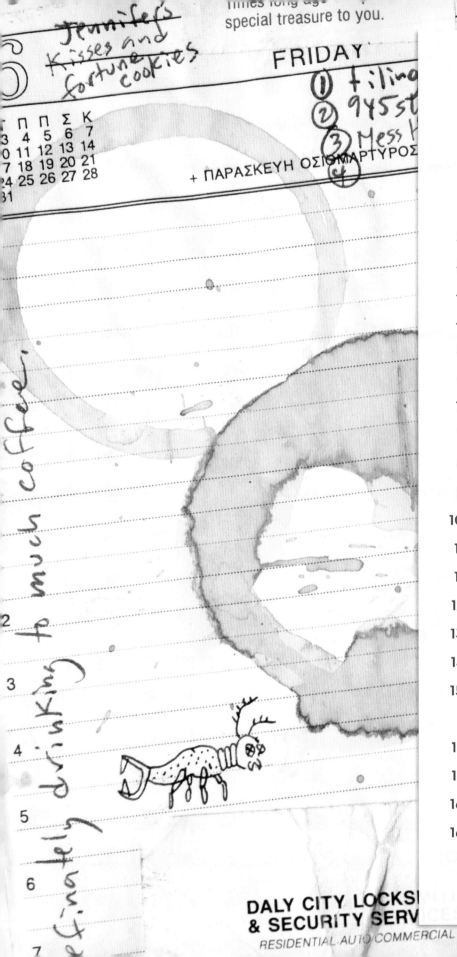

special treasure to you.

FRIDAY

① filing
② 945 st
③ Mess H
④

+ ΠΑΡΑΣΚΕΥΗ ΟΣΙΟΜΑΡΤΥΡΟΣ

Jennifer's
Kisses and
fortune cookies

Π Π Σ Κ
3 4 5 6 7
10 11 12 13 14
17 18 19 20 21
24 25 26 27 28
31

definitely drinking to much coffee.

2
3
4
5
6
7

DALY CITY LOCKSI
& SECURITY SERV
RESIDENTIAL AUTO COMMERCIAL

JULY

Contents

Introduction

Ask a room full of journalers about their reasons for keeping a journal and you will likely get no two answers that are exactly the same. Likewise, open up the journals of these artists and you'll never encounter two pages that are exactly the same.

The reasons people journal are as diverse as the marks, doodles, colors, and words that they create. On page 70, Alisa Burke explains that journaling is a "daily creative workout" that keeps her "warmed up and inspired to make art every single day." On page 118, Bruce Kremer shares that he journals "as a way to keep a visual diary" to help him catalogue objects and note observations that he deems special. "My journal is a stew of notations," he says.

Journal It! presents the fascinating *whys* and the signature *hows* of 19 tremendously talented artists who keep journals. They are: **Julie Fei-Fan Balzer**, **Jill K. Berry**, **Sarah Atwater Bourne**, **Alisa Burke**, **Debra Cooper**, **Belinda Fireman**, **Bob Fisher**, **Susanna Gordon**, **Bruce Kremer**, **Kathrin Jebsen-Marwedel**, **Corey Moortgat**, **Melanie Mowinski**, **Zom Osborne**, **Jeanette Sclar**, **Carolyn Sewell**, **Susan Shelley**, **Roben-Marie Smith**, **Anna-Maria Wolniak**, and **Alison Worman**.

For people who have yet to begin journaling, for fear of making a mistake or not knowing where to start, the artists of *Journal It!*

provide sage advice and methods on how to combat the inner critic and just get started. Says Julie Fei-Fan Balzer: "My advice … is to ruin the page. Throw black ink all over it. Rip it in half. Once it's ruined, all you have to do is rescue it (page 15)."

Each featured artist within *Journal It!* provides detailed instruction for his or her signature journaling techniques. From paints to pencils, packing tape to encaustic crayons, rubber stamps and more, you are bound to encounter methods that will undoubtedly ignite *your why* as you enter the wondrous world of visual journaling.

Especially after preparing this book, I have come to value the process of studying and observing my surroundings. Journaling allows me to be a good observer and it allows me the opportunity to better react, respond, and relate to all that is around me. And by learning the methods so generously taught by the artists convened in this book, I know that I am on the road to becoming a better journaler, better artist, and better traveler along this journey of life.

Jenny Doh

Bob Fisher

www.sketchbob.com

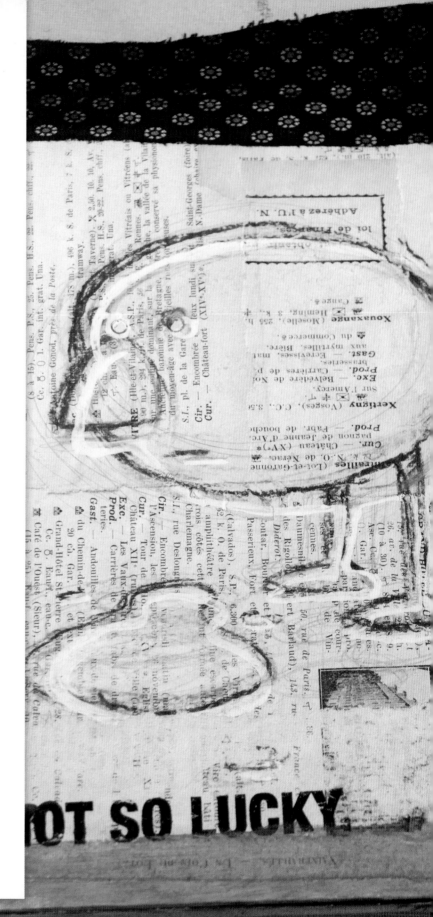

A sketchbook is arguably *the most effective tool* an artist has in the early stages of the creative process, and the discipline of *regular journaling* is a fulfilling way to grow as a creative person. I use my sketchbooks as a repository, laboratory, and playground. Here is where I can collect and store ideas, sources of inspiration, and information; *experiment* with new materials, techniques, and styles; and refine raw ideas until they are ready to be expressed in a more finished form.

I have no idea if what I make will be important to anyone in the future. I simply feel compelled to make things, especially in my sketchbooks, and that reason alone keeps me going.

COMPLETELY FREE

Over time I've learned to be creative despite fears of falling short of my artistic goals. Though I still have those feelings, I find the key to overcoming fear is twofold: realizing it for what it is, and defeating it through daily practice. Action is the antidote. Daily practice in an environment safe from judgment gives an artist the space to experiment, learn, and grow. You can choose to make your sketchbook as private or public as you wish, which removes the pressures of meeting unrealistic expectations and being compared to others. Your sketchbook can be as informal or formal as you like. If you are not satisfied with something you've made in it, you can paint over it or turn the page and work on something else. You are completely free.

OPPOSITE

After drawing with a brown water-soluble crayon, the image was drawn again, slightly overlapping, with white gouache. This method adds movement and playfulness to the image.

ABOVE

Adhering bits of assorted paper ephemera is a great way to create an instant background.

LEFT

To make a bold statement, consider making a drawing that takes up an entire spread, rather than just one page or a part of a page.

Mélangeur

When I begin a page or a spread, my first goal is to break through the barrier of the clean, white paper. I focus only on building an interesting surface texture that will serve as a base for the piece. As I continue to work the surface, I often see shapes or images suggested in the textures I've created—much like seeing figures in the clouds—and I'll record them. If a phrase pops into my head at any time, I'll record that too, taking care to treat the words as visual elements. I don't consciously compose anything until after I'm satisfied with the surface. As I near the end of the process, I am more aware of creating a balanced composition of colors, images, and lines.

fig. A

fig. B

WHAT YOU'LL NEED

* Large watercolor book
* Pages from old books
* PH-neutral PVA adhesive
* Acrylic paints
* Paintbrushes
* Pastel sticks
* Archival ink pens (regular and brush tip)
* Image
* Colorless blender
* Spoon or bone folder
* White gesso
* Water-soluble crayons

TECHNIQUE

1. Adhere pieces of book pages onto the journal with adhesive. Let dry.

2. Add strokes of acrylic paint in assorted colors. Let dry **(fig. A)**.

3. Continue to build the background:
   * Sketch objects and doodles with pastel sticks.
   * Add small marks and letters with the ink pens.
   * Add more strokes of color, painted objects, and patterns with coordinating colors of acrylic paints.

4. Select an image and make a toner-based copy of the image either on a laser printer or at a copy center that has toner-based copy machines. Transfer the toner-based copy by placing the image side of the copy onto the journal page and rubbing the back side of the copy with a colorless blender. Burnish with a spoon or bone folder and remove the copy to reveal the transfer **(fig. B)**.

5. Add another layer of strokes of color, painted objects, and patterns with assorted mediums, including white gesso and water-soluble crayons.

6. Add hand lettering with Micron pens.

Across the Plains

I filled the pages with handwritten notes, then created an abstract composition of shapes with a brush and ink. Watercolor, gouache, and gesso were used to add color and build interesting texture. Collage elements were added, and then pen and ink were used to delineate images suggested by the abstract shapes. I traced my hand and completed the composition with watercolor and colored pencil by developing shapes that overlap the figure and also serve as a background.

10,000 HOURS

Here are my top five practical and tangible pieces of advice for people interested in keeping a sketchbook or journal:

Commit to daily practice. In his book *The Outliers: The Story of Success*, Malcolm Gladwell wrote about Swedish psychologist Anders Ericsson's 10,000-hour rule, which refers to the length of time required to master a craft. That sounds like a lot (and it is), but you can master drawing and painting if you are willing to put in a bit of time every day.

Make your sketchbook a safe place. Celebrate your successes and forgive your mistakes. Don't worry about what others or your inner critic think. Enjoy the process of making things and growing as an artist.

Develop helpful habits and rituals. Use journaling to learn the vagaries of your creative process. Develop rituals and habits that inspire you and trigger your creative productivity.

Practice composing every page. So many beginning journalers focus on learning to draw or paint without taking into account how they are arranging the visual elements on their pages. Get into the habit of making a good composition each time you complete a page in your book.

Take advantage of limitations. Use prompts to give yourself assignments. It's easier to create when you have goals and constraints.

INSIGHT

I rarely have a plan when I begin a page. I generally create random lines, shapes, and textures, then allow the shapes to suggest forms that I develop into something recognizable. So, in a way, the entire beginning part of my process is trying to create those happy accidents that result in a good image.

Julie Fei-Fan Balzer

www.balzerdesigns.typepad.com

For me, my art journal *satisfies* two very important *needs:* 1) The need to keep a diary, and 2) the need to experiment with art supplies. My art journal is a *low-pressure* place to experiment and *play*. And because I don't usually share my pages publicly, I let all my *true feelings spill* onto the pages and just run free.

OPPOSITE

By creating a large flower on a spread, I found that its components allow for journaling to be compartmentalized. It is an effective method for journaling a collection of smaller ideas: sub-categories of an overall theme.

RIGHT

Strokes of watercolors were added to this free-motion stitched face made of muslin, batting, and muslin layers. This mini art quilt was attached, along with other small watercolored and stitched circles, to adorn a journal's cover.

BELOW

By leaving a large open space with just a touch of watercolor at the bottom, this page invites a longer journal entry without sub-categories.

RUIN AND RESCUE

My advice for anyone who feels gripped by fear or hesitation when looking at a blank white page is to ruin the page. Seriously. Do something to totally ruin the page. Throw black ink all over it. Rip it in half. Once it's ruined, all you have to do is rescue it. And that feels so much friendlier than starting a masterpiece on a blank page.

Watercolor and Bold Painted Words

Watercolor is a great medium for blending because it just flows together so easily. Virtually no skill required! I use it for prepping backgrounds, shading faces, doing all sorts of things. Once you create a watercolor background, there's nothing like adding bold handwriting to make the page come alive. You don't have to be an expert calligrapher to create gorgeous painted words.

It's so easy to confuse bravery with cowardice when we disapprove of the brave choice

—JULIE FEI-FAN BALZER

fig. A

fig. B

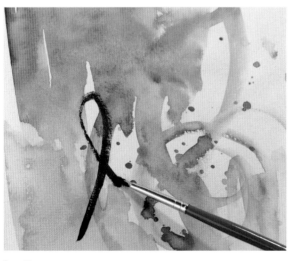

fig. C

WHAT YOU'LL NEED

* Journal
* Watercolor paints (either pans or tubes)
* Broad-tip natural paintbrush
* Water
* Palette
* Black fluid acrylic paint
* Very small paintbrush (size 0 or 1)

TECHNIQUE

1. Without wetting the page, load watercolor paint onto a broad-tip natural paintbrush and apply strokes to your page. I chose yellow for my first color.

2. Clean your brush and then load it with a second color; I used red. Apply strokes of this second color to your page and let them flow into the first color.

3. Clean your brush and then load it with a third color; I used blue. Apply strokes of this third color to your page and let them flow into the other two colors **(fig. A)**.

4. Clean your brush and then load it with watercolor. Bring the brush close to the page and shake it so paint splatters onto the page. These splats will fade into the existing paint as it dries **(fig. B)**.

5. Add more layers of different colors of paint until the page gets filled with the amount of color that you like. Use plenty of water to allow everything to flow together. Add more paint splats along the way. Allow the page to dry.

6. With a very small paintbrush and black fluid acrylic paint, add text to the watercolor background. Hold the brush like a pencil fairly close to the end and use very light pressure on the tip of the brush. Don't be afraid to go big with the letters. Handwriting looks super cool in journals when it's supersized in paint **(fig. C)**!

Held Captive

After painting and collaging this page, I hated it. I left it alone for a few weeks and then came back and gessoed over the entire page. Some of the collage came through the gesso and that was fine with me. I left the gessoed page alone for a month or two and then eventually peeled off a few of the collaged papers, which revealed some of the underlying page. I drew the pod shapes with a china marker and painted the stripes and the red outline. Next came adding the black details, and then filling in the black circles with white gesso. I used a nib pen and India ink to draw the massive text you see scrawled across the page, and finished by adding some stream-of-consciousness journaling.

INSIGHT

This page turned out nothing like I expected it to, in any way, shape, or form. My original page was a very linear piece with lots of collage and spray ink. When at first I didn't like how it was going and I took another try at it, I ended up reaching for one of my go-to shapes: pods. Sometimes when I'm stuck I just start sketching something comfortable and familiar and everything evolves from there.

Playwrights often talk about how, when they are writing a play, the characters start talking to them and dictating the story. I feel like this page sort of decided what it wanted to be. Rather than forcing the original idea that wasn't working, I just followed along with the direction that the page was taking as I let go of preconceptions and just allowed everything to be.

Sometimes I Feel Confused

I drew the faces with charcoal and let them sit for a while. I like to work in layers, and rarely sit down and complete a page from start to finish. If I do, I tend to not like it that much. Over time, I painted the watercolor stripes across the bottom of the spread, journaled, and collaged the features onto the drawings. To finish, I painted the large sentiment and added the paint splats.

Sometimes I feel confused

EXAMINE, EXPERIMENT, EMERGE

This may sound counterintuitive, but I think authenticity begins with copying, as you examine the artists you love and experiment with what they do best. By forcing yourself to really break down the things you're attracted to, you'll learn a lot about your own style. And by trying out someone else's favorite supplies, chances are good that you'll find a few of your own. Start to take what you've learned and put your own spin on it. After some time, you will find that your authentic voice starts to emerge. In order to encourage that voice to stick around, you need to kick the judgmental voice out—the one that says, "That's ugly," or "That's not good enough." That voice tries to force you to do things just like everyone else. Don't listen. Walk to the beat of your own drummer!

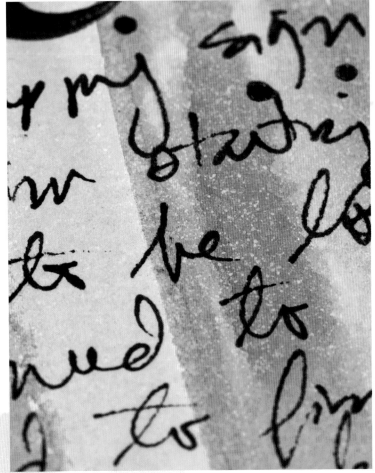

Belinda Fireman
www.belindafireman.com

Journaling allows me to *create bright, bold, colorful pages* that I enjoy looking at and touching. I always buy cheaper books so I can get that *crunchy-page feel!* Through the process of experimenting with colors and shapes on my journal pages, I *discover new ideas* that I can use in my paintings and I heighten my overall awareness of my environment and myself. My journals also allow me a space to deal with and document emotions and physical discomforts related to my spinal disc problem.

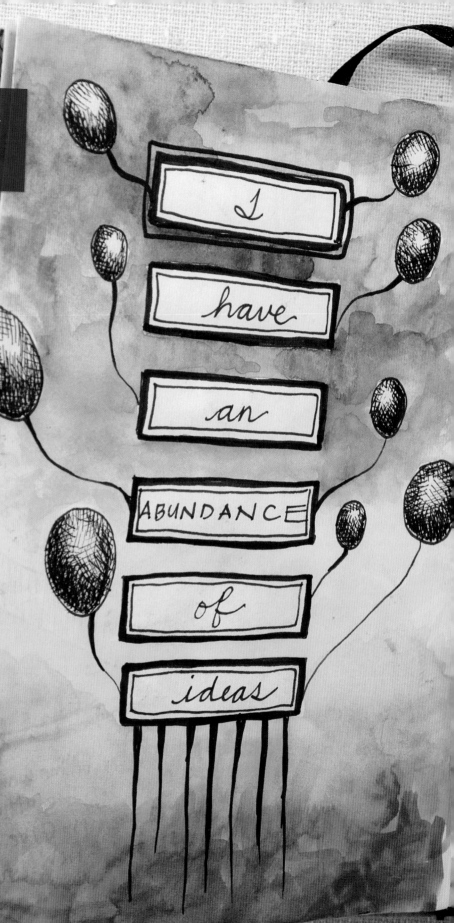

OPPOSITE

For this page, the boxes, lettering, and other pen work was done first. Water was applied to the negative space, followed by an application of watercolors in red, orange, yellow, green, blue, and purple.

LEFT

Adding strokes of gray watercolors to create shading to objects creates a sense of overall depth and dimension.

BELOW

By adding strokes of white acrylic paint over the layers of color, the energy of the page changes from calm to urgent.

CONQUERING FEAR

As a recovering perfectionist, I have experienced the fear of starting something that may not turn out perfectly. To combat this type of fear, I breathe and remind myself that it's just a piece of paper! The world will not end if I am not happy with the page. If you experience this type of fear, I challenge you to take a black marker or pen (not a pencil, because then you might be tempted to erase your "mistakes") and make a mark. Any mark. Close your eyes if you have to. Then make another mark, and then another, and see where it takes you. Remember to not judge your work so harshly.

Impulse and Intuition: Color-Mixing

With an intuitive color-mixing technique and repetitive line drawing of a simple shape, you can create a spread that creates a surprisingly bold impact. The reason I call the process "intuitive" is because it is not a precise method. You sort of have to roll with it. I love the look of the images spilling off the page. It gives the impression that there is more than meets the eye. Naturally you can use whatever colors you like, but I'll give instructions based on my process.

dreams

impulse.

intuition

fig. A

WHAT YOU'LL NEED

* ❋ Journal
* ❋ Black fine-tip marker
* ❋ Acrylic paints in assorted complementary colors
* ❋ Paintbrush
* ❋ Palette

TECHNIQUE

1. Draw a shape toward the bottom of the right side of the journal spread with a black fine-tip marker. I made a circle, but a square, star, or any simple free-form shape would work just as well. Draw a slightly larger shape around the first shape. Continue drawing larger shapes so that each ring is slightly larger than the previous one **(fig. A)**.

2. Paint the first shape with acrylic paint in the color of your choice. Clean the paintbrush with water and then paint the next shape with a second color. From this point on, do not clean the paintbrush as you transition from color to color **(fig. B)**.

3. Add a touch of white to this second color and paint the next shape. Add more white for the shape after that and so on, until you have painted the number of shapes you want in this color.

4. Without cleaning the paintbrush, dip the brush into a third color and white paint to create a faint shade for the next shape. Then add more of this third color to paint the next shape a slightly darker shade. Continue in this manner as you transition between your chosen colors. Because this method is one where you don't clean the paintbrush from color to color, you will occasionally get streaks of previous colors mixing with new colors.

5. Allow the paint to dry for at least one full day before drawing over the paint with a black fine-tip marker. When drawing with a fine-tip marker, use light pressure to avoid digging into the paint.

6. Add journaling to the negative space of the spread with a black fine-tip marker.

fig. B

Squiggle Preparation:
Watercolor Wash and Salt

After creating four small circles to hold my minimal journaling, I used watercolors and salt to create a cloudy and slightly speckled effect for the background. I didn't intend for the drawing on the other side of this page to show through, but I like the resulting depth and texture that it adds to the page.

fig. A

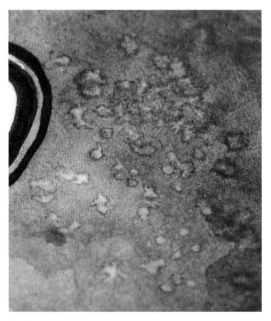

fig. B

WHAT YOU'LL NEED

* Journal
* Black chisel-tip marker
* Black fine-tip marker
* Watercolors in assorted complementary colors
* Paintbrush
* Water
* Palette
* Salt
* Paper towel

TECHNIQUE

1. Draw small shapes on the page using a chisel-tip marker. I made a circle, but a square, star, or any free-form shape would work just as well. Use a fine-tip marker to make a thin outline around your shape. Allow your lines to be imperfect and slightly wonky. Draw wonky lines from the top of the page to each of the circles with a chisel-tip marker **(fig. A)**.

2. Apply washes of watercolors in assorted shades to the negative space of the page. Allow the colors to bleed into one another.

3. To get the spotted effect shown **(fig. B)**, sprinkle salt onto the wet watercolors and allow the page to dry. Wipe off the salt with a paper towel. Note: The faint swirly motif on the page is an unintended effect caused by a doodled motif made on the other side of the page.

Mind Spew: Blended Background

The background for this page was created by blending different colors of acrylic paint. In this case, I used yellow, green, blue, and white. It is a great backdrop for journaling, and I love the bold look of the chisel-tip marker on the acrylic paint.

even
now!

i am?

but!
but!

wanted to put it out there because that's what came up for me. i know I cant just be friends with people that i choose - it takes 2 - we may not click or connect on a friend level - but see, what's the point of all this chatter? its a dream, and obviously i dont expect it to come true, but that's sort of sad, too, isn't it? i will be open to it and open to the possibility of just meeting and maybe we aren't supposed to be friends. ok - here's the thing - why do i want this? (does this even matter? what am i analyzing this for? wow, my mind does spew useless stuff sometimes). But anyway... i really admire them and can see having really fascinating conversations. Like when i met Mandy - i thought she was über-cool. i admired her strength and individuality. i dont think i really put it into words at the time, but i probably dreamed of being her friend, too. And now, she's one of my best friends. Well, i like the idea of being really honest by posting what i did and i am getting lots of great responses. im also getting better at holding my tongue. just have to walk away sometimes. im not sure what was up with my massive sugar intake last night - broke my own rule. I should really just brush my teeth after dinner and be done with it! i hope the doctor can figure out why o has such a persistent cough. i guess we'll see today.

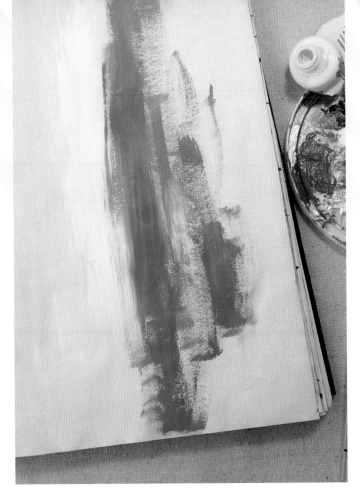

fig. A

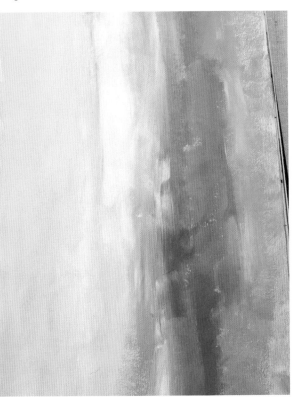

fig. B

WHAT YOU'LL NEED

* Journal
* Acrylic paints in three or four coordinating colors
* Paintbrush
* Palette
* Black chisel-tip marker
* Black fine-tip marker

TECHNIQUE

1. With various colors of acrylic paints, lay down vertical strokes of color onto the page using a paintbrush. Overlap the colors in some areas to better blend them together **(fig. A)**.

2. Use a blend of all colors to completely fill in the background. Use white paint to help soften and blend one color into another, and to help integrate the entire page **(fig. B)**. Allow the paint to dry for a full day.

3. Create horizontal lines with a black chisel-tip marker. Play with the angle of the pen while drawing, to vary the thickness of the lines.

4. Journal in between the lines using a black fine-tip marker.

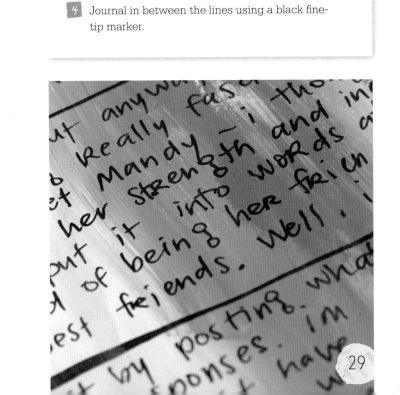

WORKING like this reminds me of high school art. So much effort that i would put into my drawings, especially cross-hatching. The more i do, the more i [thi]nk i have to do. i am starting to feel the weight of this deadline. [ke]ep thinking of the "gentle hum of anxiety" - perfect music for how [it] feels. interesting how, with a looming deadline, the [first] to go are the things that take care of me - [exerc]ise. it's only today that i have skipped, but [meditati...] first

30

13377

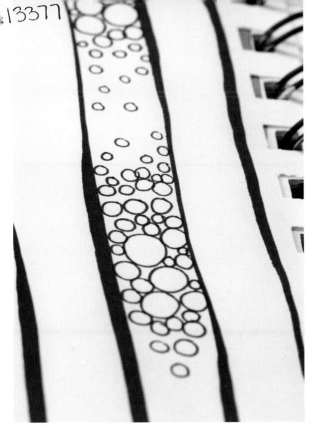

Bubbly Obsession

I used a black chisel-tip marker to draw horizontal lines, allowing the lines to vary in thickness. Next, I drew small circles in the space between two of the lines, using a black fine-tip marker. I filled in the negative space with the marker and repeated this process on other sections, then added journaling and doodling to complete the page.

INSIGHT

Never before had I spent the kind of time that I did to create this page. In some ways, it felt like it was a waste of time—if I was putting this amount of effort into it, then it should be a drawing outside of my journal. But I also liked demonstrating to myself that I have the capacity for commitment and perseverance. Focusing on a drawing like this was also good meditative practice for me.

ACCEPTING ONE'S STYLE

Acceptance is an important ingredient to discovering one's style. For about a year, I couldn't stop drawing spheres. I wanted to change that, because I thought they were getting old and boring, but then I realized that they were just part of my style. Once I was able to accept that, the spheres eventually morphed into something else. I also used to berate myself for always using such bright colors. I have finally accepted that bright colors are part of who I am as an artist—they are part of my signature look!

Debra Cooper

www.debracooperart.com

When I first started journaling, I loved the idea of having *a special place for my art* that would be just for me. I was doing a lot of design work at the time and struggled a lot with comparing my work with that of other artists. I decided my art journal would be the place where I would give myself permission to create whatever I felt inspired to *create without judging* it as good or bad.

At first I had to shut out the inner critic that tried to tell me that what I made wasn't good enough, but the more often I worked in my journal, the easier it became to experiment and even fail. The irony was that instead of making lots of pages I was unhappy with, *I became more confident* in my own instincts as an artist.

ENJOY THE PROCESS

When faced with a creative block, I always try to get started with something that comes easy for me or some technique I am comfortable with. I push the thoughts of the end product out of my mind and try to enjoy the process of creating by just getting some color onto the page. Nothing inspires me more than smearing color over paper or canvas. First I pick a color that I really love and just squirt the paint right onto the paper. Then I scrape it around a bit with a palette knife, then add some more paint in another color. I keep going until swirling colors together has warmed up the creative juices and the ideas begin to flow.

OPPOSITE

The key to adding layers of color is allowing each layer to dry. This will prevent incompatable colors from blending together and accidentally becoming mud-like.

ABOVE

Partially scraping paint over a drawing is a terrific way to make the different parts of the drawing appear to be resting on various planes.

LEFT

Once a page is filled with scraped colors of paint, it's fun to isolate a portion with doodles that can encapsulate the journaling.

Debra Cooper   33

Scrape and Doodle

The key to this technique is to not allow the first scraped paint to fully dry before you scrape the second color of paint. As one color touches the other, they mix and create a very interesting effect. The other key is to scrape paint directly over the doodles and lettering, which allows the piece to gain added depth.

fig. A

fig. B

* Journal
* Acrylic craft paint in four coordinating colors
* Palette knife (or old gift card or other scraper)
* Black waterproof ink pen

TECHNIQUE

1. Squirt a few drops of paint directly onto the journal page. Scrape the paint over the surface using a palette knife. Make sure to not cover the entire page and to pull some of the paint all the way to the edge of the paper **(fig. A)**.

2. Squirt a few drops of a second color of paint onto the page without waiting for the first color to dry. This will allow the two colors to mix together as they overlap.

3. Repeat this step with a third and fourth color of acrylic paint until the entire page is covered with scraped paint. Allow the page to dry **(fig. B)**.

4. Doodle and journal with a black waterproof pen. Mix in some unique hand lettering and combine words and images for a more intricate design.

5. Squirt a few drops of one of the paint colors you used directly onto your palette knife. Scrape this paint over portions of the doodling and journaling to create a multilayered effect. Continue with more paint until the pen work is integrated into the entire design.

Stencil and Spray

This technique takes advantage of the interesting way that water-soluble spray inks interact with acrylic paint. The sprays used here are Ranger Adirondack Color Washes. When you apply inexpensive acrylic paint (or any water-based paint) over the top of the ink, the vivid pigment breaks through in a beautiful way that can be manipulated for amazing results. When using these spray inks, I recommend that you spray the journal inside a large box or outdoors, as the pigment really flies and can cover your work surface rather quickly. However, the ink can be easily cleaned up with a damp rag, even after it has dried.

WHAT YOU'LL NEED

* Journal
* Spray ink in at least two colors
* Stencils or masks (see Stencils and Masks Defined, page 39)
* Scrap paper
* Brayer (optional)
* Paper towels
* Acrylic craft paint, two colors and white
* Palette knife or other paint scraper
* Short bristled paintbrush

TECHNIQUE

1. Lay a stencil or mask onto a scrap piece of paper and spray well with one color of spray ink. Carefully remove the stencil or mask from the scrap paper, turn it over, and press lightly onto the surface of the journal page. You may want to place a scrap piece of paper over the back of the stencil and then rub or brayer over it lightly. Peel back the stencil or mask from the page and set aside. Allow the page to dry **(fig. A)**.

2. Squirt a few drops of one acrylic paint color directly onto your journal page, on top of the stenciled design. Scrape the paint with a palette knife to cover the entire page. Allow to dry **(fig. B)**.

3. Lay the stencil back over the journal page, lining it up to cover the stenciled design. Lightly mist the stencil with a second color of spray ink, then carefully remove the wet stencil and set aside. It will take longer for the ink to dry where it lands on top of the paint because it cannot be so easily absorbed into the paper. You may also use a paper towel to blot puddles of ink where necessary. If some of the spray ink lands outside of the stenciled area, just rub the ink with a damp paint rag to remove it **(fig. C)**.

4. Dry-brush a second color of paint around the outside of the stenciled design to the edge of the page with a stippling motion, using a bristled paintbrush. Allow patches of the color underneath to show through for added depth.

5. For a mottled look, use a dry brush to lightly stipple white paint on top of the second acrylic color, leaving patches of color showing through.

6. Use a pencil or pen to highlight the edges of the stenciled design.

7. Journal on top of or around the edges of the stenciled design to complete the page.

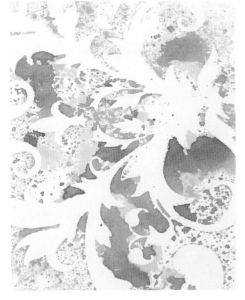

fig. A

fig. B

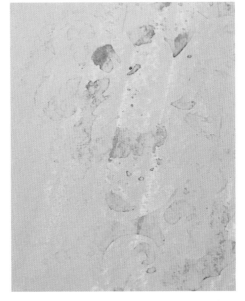

fig. C

My Impossible Dream

After scraping acrylic paints across the page, I misted the scraped paint with spray inks. I then sprayed the page with water to allow the colors to blend and drip together.

INSIGHT

After doodling a bit onto the painted paper, I felt the page had a dreamlike quality about it. I chose the words "my impossible dream" to reflect that. My doodles are a kind of personal imaginative flower, which I contrasted with a more realistic drawing of a flower cut from a piece of scrapbook paper.

my
impossible
dream

STENCILS AND MASKS DEFINED

A stencil is a thin sheet of material with a design cut out from it. When you place a stencil onto a piece of paper, you can apply paint, ink, or other substance into the cut-out section to make the design appear on the paper.

A mask is the negative part of the stencil, the part that has been cut out. When you place a mask onto a piece of paper, you can apply paint, ink, or other substance around the edges to make the space around the cut-out section appear on the paper.

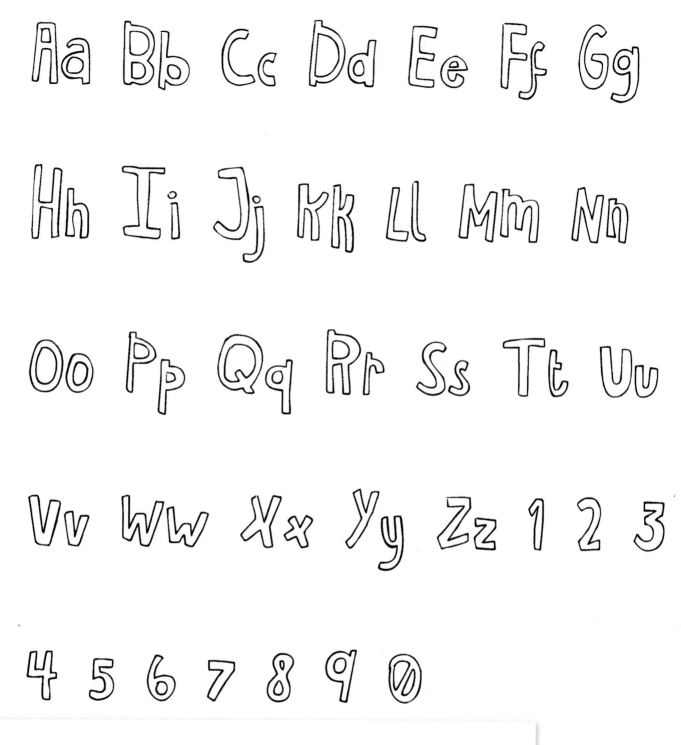

CREATING CUSTOM ALPHABETS

I love to add hand lettering because it makes the journal page or spread become even that much more meaningful. As you observe the different fonts around you, try your own hand at creating a font, and practice drawing that font in both upper and lower case. Once you develop a set that you like, create it in one sheet and refer back to it when you want to add that lettering to a page. Here is a set that I've drawn which you can use as inspiration as you create your own.

Her Voice is Living

This spread was created by first scraping various colors of acrylic paints across the page. Once all the layers were dry, I drew the flowers, made the doodles, and then added the journaling. I scraped additional paint over some of the doodles to add depth.

INSIGHT

This spread contains a line from a poem by Ovid, the Roman poet, something I had been reading with my children. "But all may hear her for her voice is living ... " I think that is a lovely line, as it reminds me of the special time I had with my kids, reading poetry.

Carolyn Sewell
carolynsewell.com

I've always had a terrible memory, so at a young age, I started *sketching notes* and doodles in my books to help me *visualize* the information that I *struggled to memorize*. I doubt I would've graduated high school, let alone college, without this technique. And since my memory hasn't improved, I continue to take visual notes at design lectures and conferences. I've always said that my pen is my *hearing aid*. I can't listen without it.

OPPOSITE

Journaling does not mean that only one type of font or lettering belongs on a page. Mixing things up by creating assorted experimental lettering and doodling adds great interest to a page.

LEFT

Dots are cool! They can add a pattern to letters while allowing white space to surround the dots, causing the page to feel more fluid and open.

BELOW

When there is a story to tell, or if there are just way too many thoughts happening at once, creating small boxes on a page is a great way to capture the scenes of a story, or scenes from separate stories.

WHEN I'M STUCK

A blank page is terrifying enough, but a book full of them is almost paralyzing. My two suggestions for dealing with this come from the amazing designer and illustrator Frank Chimero:

* Don't use precious materials. The more you treasure a tool, the less likely you are to use it.

* Scribble all over the first page, because there's no way you can make anything worse than that.

My Process

Journals are where I do my thinking and processing. Whether I'm listening to a lecture, observing something or someone, or just doing stream-of-consciousness journaling, I basically let it all come out and then pretty up what has come out with my pen. To do all that, I just need two things: a large sketchbook and a black gel pen. That's it.

INCORPORATE THE GOOF

Perfection is overrated and exhausting. I have typos and botched ideas all through my journals, but instead of abandoning the entire page, I try to incorporate the goof, or at least work around it.

INSIGHT

These five pages were made during a lecture by Stefan Sagmeister. I took quick notes and then shaded and darkened my notes later. I don't sketch with a pencil when taking notes; instead, I try to capture all the highlights of the presentation, then worry about making it pretty later.

Not only does Stefan speak very quickly, but everything he says is quotable and awesome, so my fingers were on fire trying to keep up. I do wish I had done a better representation of the "cake of happiness."

OBSESSIONS MAKE MY LIFE WORSE AND MY WORK BETTER

STYLE THAT FITS YOUR PERSONALITY

I don't care how much you love the look of calligraphy; if the pen doesn't feel right in your hand and you're not enjoying yourself, then it's not the style for you. If you're journaling while commuting on a bus, then watercolor may not be for you. You have to find the tools that feel right and a style that fits your personality and lifestyle. Once you figure that out, your voice has nowhere to go but through your work, and that will always be authentic.

Listening to the POLICE ON A MOTORCYCLE IN AUSTRIA

HAPPINESS TO STEFAN MUH-ZOOM

Designers that make me happy:
• JAMES TURRELL (fake skies)
• Ji Lee (speech bubbles)
• ANISH KAPOOR (metal bubble sculpture)

COMPLAINING IS SILLY, EITHER ACT OR FORGET.

DO MORE OF THE THINGS I LIKE AND FEWER OF THE THINGS I DON'T LIKE

ASSUMING IS STIFLING

what does an (') apostrophe do? it kills a letter! (re: apostrophe gun illo for paper co.)

Anna-Maria Wolniak

www.annamariawolniak.wordpress.com

The creation of my journals is driven exclusively by my *emotional needs*. There are times in my life when I am *incapable of conveying* the emotions or thoughts within me. Or perhaps during these times, there is no person able to understand me or what I am going through. In such moments, I start painting. I don't feel the need to create large paintings. *I prefer smaller expressions* that I can make in my journals.

I have seen the SEA when it is STORMY and wild, when it is quiet and serene; when it is DARK and moody, and all its moods, I see MYSELF

MORE OR LESS

Some people say "less is more." And others say "more is more." I actually say "more or less." In other words, do and express exactly as much or as little as you reckon is appropriate. There was a time when I really wanted to master the art of minimalism with its pure and restrained form. No matter how hard I tried, I failed completely. I believe that each artist should adjust and adapt, according to his or her unique preference. I think the journal should be entirely "yours" and genuine. Nothing should inhibit you—neither the format, the technique, the subject, nor philosophies like "less is more" or "more is more."

When words become unclear, I shall FOCUS with PHOTOGRAPHS. When images become inadequate I shall be content with... SILENT.

breathe

I'm glad that you HERE...

OPPOSITE

After paint is put on a page, there are many directions in which you can take it. On this page, a small black-and-white photo and scraps of paper were adhered with masking tape. Pencil scribbles were added, and journaling with a combination of pencil and rubber stamp work complete the page.

ABOVE

Here is a page that includes splatters of paint and blotches of ink ... things that imperfectly complete the page.

LEFT

Using a single rubber stamp image, like the one of the birdcage used on this page, can add instant whimsy and playfulness.

Watercolor Clouds

When I discovered watercolor, I found it to be the one and only art medium that allowed me to express my emotions onto paper without having to plan or think too much. With watercolor, I can create instinctively, rapidly, and impulsively. Sometimes, when I look at the pages created in this manner, I am surprised at what comes out of me. This is the wonder and magic of watercolor.

WHAT YOU'LL NEED

* Journal pages
* Soft, natural paintbrushes: Broad tip (for applying larger quantities of paint); Round pointed tip (for painting details); Broad flat tip (for filling larger planes with color)
* Watercolor pan paints (any ordinary basic set of classic colors)
* Palette
* Water
* Pencil
* Rubber stamps
* Inkpad
* Small, hard, artificial paintbrush (for splashing paint)
* Photos and/or magazine clippings
* Masking tape
* Paper ephemera
* Black ink
* Dip pen
* Watercolor crayons

TECHNIQUE

fig. A

1   Dip the broad tip paintbrush with water and paint the paper with the water. Paint quickly and randomly the portion of paper where you want the paint to land (**fig. A**).

2   While the paper is wet, dip the paintbrush into watercolor paint (your color of choice) and gently apply it to the paper. The paint will begin to spread to wherever the water has been painted (**fig. B**).

3   Allow this first color to dry a little bit. Apply more water to the paper quickly and randomly, and apply a second color, using the same method. By allowing the first color to dry before moving to the second color, you will prevent the colors from fully blending together. This is useful when you want to place blue and yellow next to each other, but do not want to have the two blend to create a green. However, if you do want a blended green to appear, the second color can be added without the first one being fully dried (**fig. C**).

fig. B

4   After the background is dry, add journaling with a pencil and/or rubber stamps. Add blotches and blobs in varying sizes (see Blotches and Blobs on page 53).

5   Attach small photos or magazine clippings with pieces of masking tape. I also like to use masking tape as a design element by placing small pieces in selected spots of the page.

6   Add bold circles or other random marks with black ink and a dip pen.

7   Add circles or other random marks with watercolor crayons. Blend these marks by brushing over them with water.

fig. C

Piece by Piece

Here is a spread that was inspired by the image of the woman standing in nature. The colors in the image are the ones I re-created with watercolors to fill the rest of the spread. When working with an inspired image, it's alright not to have everything planned out but to allow one stroke to inform the next stroke, and eventually the entire spread. Step by step, piece by piece.

ink. I FEEL

Sunday

monday, tuesday...

Piece by piece
is how I'll let go of you....
kiss by kiss will leave
my mind one at a time...
one att a time
one at a time....

PIECE & KISS

ORGANIC
COTTON

THIS WONDERFULLY SOFT
GARMENT IS MADE WITH
CERTIFIED ORGANIC COTTON -
COTTON THAT HAS BEEN
GROWN WITHOUT THE USE
OF HAZARDOUS CHEMICALS.
READ MORE ON
HM.COM/MATERIALS

BLOTCHES AND BLOBS

Saturated Hues. To create color blotches that take on more controlled shapes, load the paintbrush with a significant amount of watercolor and apply it directly onto dry paper **(fig. A)**.

Gentle Splash. To add little blobs of intensive color, splash the paint onto dry paper. Dip the artificial hard brush into the watercolor paint and splash the paint onto the paper by shaking the brush over the page. If the blobs become too intense, remove some of the paint while it is still wet by pressing a tissue or rag onto the page **(fig. B)**.

Smudgy Splash. Use the same method as the Gentle Splash but first moisten the base with water **(fig. C)**.

Splash. To create a larger "broken" blob, use a big round brush, moisten it with water, then load it with a significant amount of paint. Place the work on the floor and stand over it, keeping the brush high above the ground. Wait until the drop of paint falls on the base. This is a risky method as it is really hard to foresee the final place where the paint will drop, but the result is spectacular. To make the mark feather, wet the paper beforehand **(fig. D)**.

fig. A

fig. B

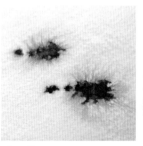

fig. C

fig. D

INSIGHT

Once the colors and imagery and photos start building a spread, there are words and thoughts that the art coaxes out of the artist. Lyrical and poetic journaling I think is most beautiful when produced in this manner.

I don't think, I FEIL

Sunday

Piece by piece
is how I'll let go of you
kiss by kiss will leave
my mind one at a time
one at a time
...one at a time

ORGANIC
COTTON

Barcelona

I view the process of journaling as an instant form of speaking my thoughts and emotions on paper. It is the only form of art that involves no planning, no wondering. Everything is created instinctively, immediately, and rapidly. The immediacy of watercolor aids in my journaling process.

PORQE me duelle el corazón porque es tan FUERTE que solo podré VIVIRTE en la distancia y escribirte una can

PORQUE me duele
el corazón porque
es tan FUERTE,
que solo podré
VIVIRTE en la
distancia y
escribirte una canción

te quiero Barcelona

Por qué tanto perderse
tanto buscarse sin
encontrarse me encierran
los muros de todas
partes BARCELONA

Te estás equivocando no
puedes seguir intentando
que el mundo sea otra
cosa y
volar
como

INSIGHT

A paper doily was adhered
to the lower portion of this
page before the painting
process. The texture is subtle
and beautiful ... even with
the cracks made into it with
simple pencil lines.

Anna-Maria Wolniak   55

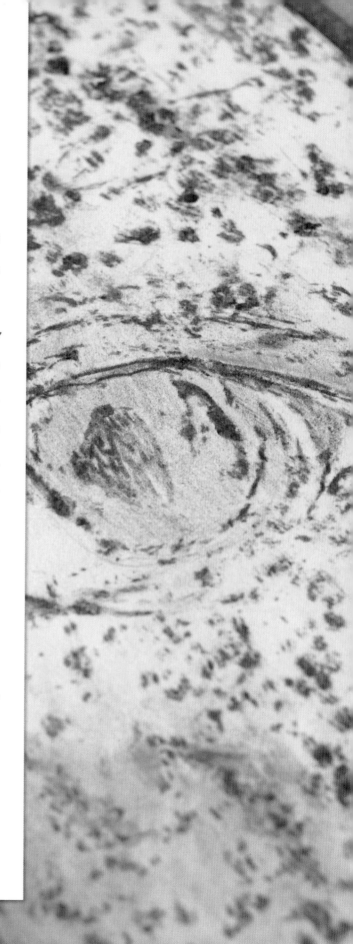

Melanie Mowinski
www.melaniemowinski.com

I make these Field Guides to Tree Rubbings as a way of *documenting time* spent in the wilderness, in the woods, or in a city park. The *trees* that I portray tend to *represent* some sort of personal experience for me, so the process becomes a metaphorical expression of me as the tree in that particular space. The Field Guides are also *memories* of special moments. I will write about memories from my youth or other periods of time that are related to that place and/or tree. This helps me resolve lingering things that I may or may not like about my life, which helps me organize them in a way that makes them more powerful, and meaningful.

The Field Guides are also *an excuse* sometimes *for being alone* in the woods. I've been making them for a number of years now. That time spent in quiet solitude in the forest *refuels* me and inspires me to live more fully with the humans in my life.

OPPOSITE

By using different colors of marking or encaustic crayons, rubbings can result in diverse and stunning effects.

LEFT

Subtle colors were added to this rubbing with colored pencils. Keeping things simple in terms of color will enhance the beauty of the rubbing.

BELOW

Where as tree rubbings allow the tree to speak, Field Guides allow the artist to speak about the details of the surroundings and process.

DO IT ANYWAY

Like most people, I've felt the fear of looking at a blank page and not knowing how to begin. Thankfully, I haven't had that feeling for a long time now, because I've gotten to a place where I know it's just a page among many and that some are going to be great, some not so great, and some I won't like at all.

My advice is to know that you are not alone in feeling that fear. And to quote Susan Jeffers, "Feel the fear and do it anyway." Every creative person I know feels fear from time to time. Sometimes it helps to practice on separate paper outside of the journal. It also helps to use journals that you aren't emotionally attached to.

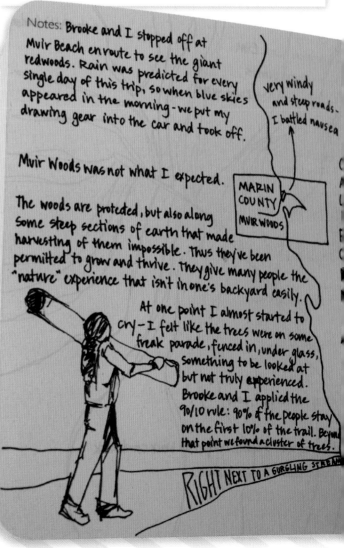

Notes: Brooke and I stopped off at Muir Beach enroute to see the giant redwoods. Rain was predicted for every single day of this trip, so when blue skies appeared in the morning - we put my drawing gear into the car and took off.

very windy and steep roads - I battled nausea

MARIN COUNTY
MUIR WOODS

Muir Woods was not what I expected.

The woods are protected, but also along some steep sections of earth that made harvesting of them impossible. Thus they've been permitted to grow and thrive. They give many people the "nature" experience that isn't in one's backyard easily.

At one point I almost started to cry - I felt like the trees were on some freak parade, fenced in, under glass, something to be looked at but not truly experienced. Brooke and I applied the 90/10 rule: 90% of the people stay on the first 10% of the trail. Beyond that point we found a cluster of trees.

RIGHT NEXT TO A GURGLING STREAM

Tree Rubbings

Tree rubbing is a process that is similar to rubbing gravestones, but more active and not as predictable. Each tree is different and some, especially the older ones, are difficult to rub. Birch, sycamore, and most very young trees make for good rubbings.

I've made at least a couple hundred tree rubbings. Some I want to add text to, either with an inkjet printer or rubber stamps; for those I add the text first, before the actual rubbing. This is because the crayons used in the rubbings act as a resist to inks. On some, after the rubbing, I like to add watercolors and colored pencils to pull out some areas and emphasize others.

Once the rubbings are completed, you can cut the papers to a desired size and make them into books or keep them as loose pages in a box. I ended up making my rubbings into simple stitched signature books, and I house them in constructed clamshell boxes.

WHAT YOU'LL NEED

* 100-percent cotton paper, lightweight, cream-colored
* Rubber stamps (optional)
* Inkpad (optional)
* Inkjet printer (optional)
* Tree
* Marking or encaustic crayon, or jumbo layout graphite stick (without the holder)
* Watercolors
* Small paintbrush
* Colored pencils

TECHNIQUE

1. If you would like to have text on the final piece, decide where that text will be positioned. Either rubber-stamp the desired text or feed the paper through an inkjet printer to print the text. This step is optional.

2. Place the paper directly onto the tree and hold it in place with one hand. Rub the paper with the edge of a crayon to create the texture on the paper **(fig. A)**.

3. Examine the rubbing and determine whether there are areas you would like to enhance or emphasize. If so, add subtle color to those spots with a touch of watercolor or colored pencils. I recommend this step be done with a very light hand so the color is not gratuitous; I like the added color to enhance the original beauty and unique features of the tree, rather than overtake them **(fig. B)**.

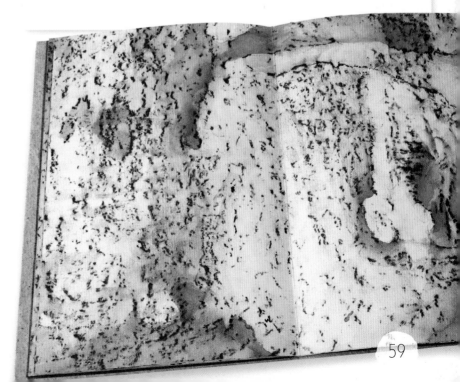

Field Guides

After I create the tree rubbings, I make small Field Guides. They are like small pamphlets that become custom journals of sorts, with each spread becoming a composition. I typically organize these by including four to six trees in most guides. I want the template pages to be personal Field Guides that not only represent the trees but also my relationship to the trees. The specific components of the template are intentionally generic—they are just an outline to help me direct my thinking and drawing when I get out into the field.

To make my custom Field Guides, I first determined what I wanted to include in the template. I tried out pencil and pen versions until I achieved the specific criteria desired. Once satisfied, I used a software program to create the title page, page spreads, and colophon. For each Field Guide, I printed out these pages and stacked them accordingly, with a piece of dyed Tyvek for the cover (see How to Dye Tyvek on opposite page).

Notes: Besides the COPSE, two WITNESS trees remain @ Gettysburg. Both are Lindens. All other trees were planted during the last century.

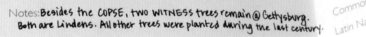

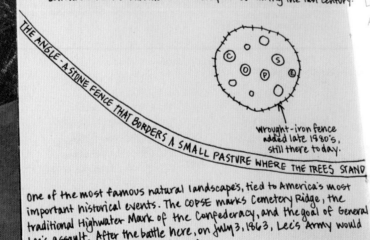

wrought-iron fence added late 1980's, still there today.

One of the most famous natural landscapes, tied to America's most important historical events. The COPSE marks Cemetery Ridge, the traditional Highwater Mark of the Confederacy, and the goal of General Lee's assault. After the battle here, on July 3, 1863, Lee's Army would never reach such a high point again.

BUT, the trees are growing: 30 feet above the original 20 feet during battle. Some preservationists want to maintain the natural landscape as it was in 1863. Trees have been removed. Pastures reestablished. The COPSE and her witness trees are hopefully safe from a return (read removal) to the war size.

Location: Gettysburg, PA The Copse of Trees

Common Name: Chestnut Oak
Latin Name: Quercus pinus
Approximate Age: 140+

Identifying Features:
Tree Shape:

Bark:

Leaf Shape:

Cone/Fruit/Flower: VERY LARGE AND SKINNY ACORN

Scars:

Date: September 11, 2006

Material: encaustic and stanol crayons
Conversation/Documentation: Park rangers - permission fenced area

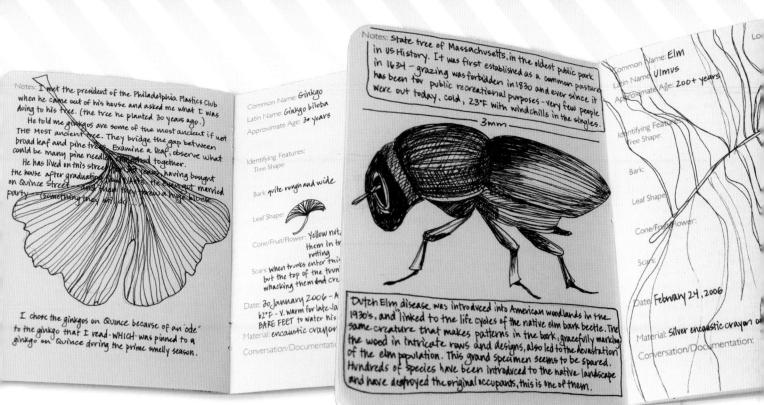

Notes: I met the president of the Philadelphia Plastics Club when he came out of his house and asked me what I was doing to his tree. (the tree he planted 30 years ago.)
He told me ginkgos are some of the most ancient if not THE MOST ancient tree. They bridge the gap between broad leaf and pine trees. Examine a leaf, observe what could be many pine needles fused together.
He has lived on this street __ years, having bought the house after graduation __ and then got married on Quince Street __ and then __ threw a huge block party __ (something they still do)

I chose the ginkgos on Quince because of an 'ode' to the ginkgo that I read · WHICH · was pinned to a ginkgo on Quince during the prime smelly season.

Common Name: Ginkgo
Latin Name: Ginkgo biloba
Approximate Age: 30 years

Identifying Features:
Tree Shape:

Bark: quite rough and wide

Leaf Shape:

Cone/Fruit/Flower: Yellow nut, __ them in th__ rotting

Scars: When trunks enter this __ but the top of the trunk __ whacking them and cre__

Date: 30 January 2006 - A__ 62°F - V. Warm for late Ja__ BARE FEET to water his __
Material: encaustic crayon

Conversation/Documentati__

Notes: State tree of Massachusetts, in the oldest public park in US History. It was first established as a common pasture in 1634 - grazing was forbidden in 1830 and ever since it has been for public recreational purposes - very few people were out today, cold, 23°F with windchills in the singles.

— 3mm —

Dutch Elm disease was introduced into American woodlands in the 1930's, and linked to the life cycles of the native elm bark beetle. The same creature that makes patterns in the bark, gracefully marking the wood in intricate rows and designs, also led to the devastation of the elm population. This grand specimen seems to be spared. Hundreds of species have been introduced to the native landscape and have destroyed the original occupants, this is one of them.

Common Name: Elm
Latin Name: Ulmus
Approximate Age: 200+ years

Identifying Feat__
Tree Shape:

Bark:

Leaf Shape:

Cone/Fr__Flower:

Scars:

Date: February 24, 2006

Material: Silver encaustic crayon o__

Conversation/Documentation:

HOW TO DYE TYVEK

Tyvek is a material made from 100-percent high-density polyethylene fibers. It is flexible but sturdy, which is why I like to use it as covers of my Field Guides. I buy mine in bulk online. The color of Tyvek is usually white or off-white. I like to dye it with acrylic inks. Here's how:

1. Lightly dampen a sponge with as many drops of ink as you need to get the desired color. The larger the size of Tyvek, the greater the amount of ink you will need on the sponge.

2. Rub the inked sponge onto the Tyvek. The ink will dry quickly and sometimes drops or strokes will remain. This can be beautiful if you want the effect of drops and strokes, but if you want an even, consistent color, you need to move quickly.

3. Once dry, cut the dyed Tyvek to size. Use it as covers for books or other projects.

TIPS

* If you want to blend colors, do the blending of the inks prior to putting it onto the sponge.

* Have fun and just squirt or drop the ink right onto the Tyvek to see what happens. The more ink you use, the more likely it will soak through to the other side, which can be good or bad, depending on what sort of effect you are trying to achieve.

* Dyeing Tyvek requires practice, patience, and experimentation.

Jill K. Berry
jillberrydesign.com

Journaling helps me take time to be in the here and now. *I notice more about my life when I journal.* I don't miss the little stuff I should be appreciating, like the color of the sky, the *pearls of wisdom* from my kids, the food on my table, *the view* from where I am sitting. In my journals, I make sketches of what I notice and the ideas that come to me. My larger art pieces usually *germinate* in my journals.

MARKS AND COFFEE STAINS

I like blank pages and it's never been my practice to "prepare" pages with backgrounds. I just jump right in. Having said that, if the blank page scares you, I have two suggestions:

* Ask a kid or some fun person to make a mark in your journal on any page. Or take the journal and spill coffee on a page. Coffee makes a pretty color. Once your pristine journal is marked it is no longer blank and scary. Make something out of the spill or the mark your friend made, and see where that leads you.

* Get a soft brush full of a color you like. Close your eyes, and listen to the sounds you hear. Guide the brush across the page in rhythm with that sound.

OPPOSITE

When you have a colored background and bold black-and-white elements, bring one of the colors forward to integrate the two palettes. I added a gold flower to the black-and-white lapel of the man to better tie the colors together.

ABOVE

Because flowers don't move around like people or animals, they are great objects to sketch. For this page, once the sketch of the daffodils was done, watercolors were added, and then a quick frame made with a thin black marker. The lettering was done with a broad-tipped black marker.

LEFT

Journaling doesn't have to be done using one single type of pen or one single type of ink. Use different nibs, colors, and styles of lettering ... even a made-up and experimental one that looks more like marks than letters.

Text Grids and Composition

I often work with lined areas in my journals, in part because it is so reminiscent of being a kid and having lined pages, and in part because I just like stripes. In a practical sense, the lines give you a specific area to fill with text, and permission to fill the outer area with whatever you like.

For this page, I started by drawing figures of Italian men. As I started adding the lines, I had to rethink the composition because my lines were forming an unattractive backward "Z" **(fig. A)**. I felt the composition needed a softer shape, so I ended up adding an arch and neutralizing the rest of the background to soften the sharp angles and call less attention to them. Then I added the lettering.

WHAT YOU'LL NEED

* Journal
* 2H Pencil
* Ruler
* Eraser
* Black-colored marking pencil
* Watercolors
* Small paintbrush
* 5mm black fine-line waterproof marker
* Small pointed calligraphy nib
* Red, blue, or green gouache, mixed with water
* Gel pens, light green and gold

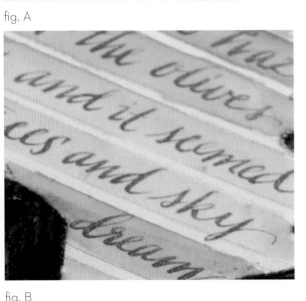

fig. A

fig. B

TECHNIQUE

1. Draw figures of people in different poses. For this page, I sketched figures of three people using my basic sketching technique (see Jill's Sketches, page 69).

2. Add lines with a pencil and ruler on a few areas of the journal page. For my page, I started on the right with the area behind the artist. The second lined area was the one above and around the umbrella man, which needed to go at a slant so it would look like rain. The third was the area at his base to form a path where he was walking (I later abandoned these lines to soften the composition) **(fig. A)**.

3. Use a small paintbrush to add watercolor washes, in coordinating shades, between the lines. Remember that you will be lettering over this, so it should not be too dark or saturated. I muted the colors behind the artist slightly by adding a tiny bit of gray to the wet bright colors before applying them to the page. The umbrella man needed watery colors for the rain coming down, so I used blues and greens.

4. Sketch an arch with the pencil, and fill in the rest of the space with neutral shades of watercolors.

5. Add text within the bands of watercolor. For the bands near the artist, I used a fine-line waterproof marker. Near the umbrella man, I used a small calligraphy nib and gouache. I used a light green gel pen to add text on the inner arch and then a gold gel pen on the exterior of the arch **(fig. B)**.

Tiger Lilies

One of my favorite possessions is a beautiful art deco vase that my late grandmother left me. I once filled this vase with tiger lilies and became inspired by the goddess nature of the figure on the vase, which was surrounded by the majestic flowers. The composition begged to be sketched, painted, and journaled, so that's what I did. I created a page with watercolors, followed by four stages and styles of lettering with different writing instruments.

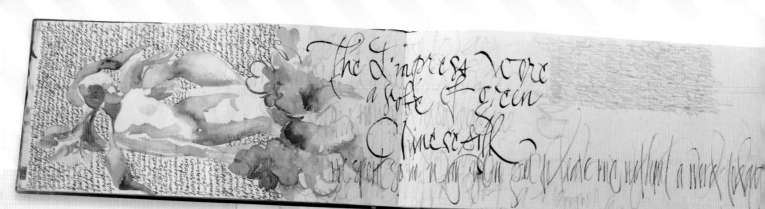

WHAT YOU'LL NEED

* Journal
* 2H Pencil
* Watercolors
* Small paintbrush
* Eraser
* Quill feather pen
* Black ink
* 5mm Micron black fine-line waterproof marker
* Felt-tipped marker, silver
* Very sharp colored pencil

TECHNIQUE

1. Sketch the focal element (in my case, the sculptural figure from the vase) with a pencil. Sketch in the details to surround the focal element.

2. Paint water onto shadow areas of your image, so the paper is damp. Load the brush with a small amount of watercolor in a color of your choice and brush it onto the damp areas. Once dry, add more of this color to areas where you want the shade to be darker. Paint the details in a similar manner with coordinating watercolors. Once dry, either leave the pencil marks or erase them with an eraser.

3. Add calligraphic lettering using a quill feather pen and black ink. You can buy quill pens at specialty pen shops or you can learn to make them with real feathers (look for tutorials online). I like working with a quill pen because it has an edge like a metal calligraphy nib, and is very flexible, so it creates more organic lines.

4. Add free-thought journaling with a black fine-line waterproof marker. Let the words wrap around the figure.

5. Add script lettering toward the bottom of the page, using a silver marker in a size between the small journaling and large calligraphic lettering. This will give weight to the page.

6. Add a final layer of compressed and elongated handwriting with a very sharp colored pencil. To achieve this type of writing, draw two faint horizontal guide lines, with a distance between them that is three times the height of your normal writing. Make your letters the same width as you normally would, but when drawing them, start at the bottom line and go all the way up to the top line. This takes some practice but not as much as you might think **(fig. A)**.

fig. A

JILL K. BERRY

Over the Top

The top of this page is continuous journaling, writing without lifting the black pen off the page. The background was done with a brush and walnut ink. A layer of walnut ink and pink watercolor were added on top.

INSIGHT

I think continuous journaling is a great exercise, especially at times when the mind is overflowing. Get it down, get it out. I did not care about reading it afterward—just the doing of it was what I needed—so I painted over the top.

JILL'S SKETCHES

The key to creating good sketches of people is to practice, practice, practice. Start by copying photos or magazine pictures and feel free to sketch or trace the outlines of the figures to get started. As you strengthen your general sketching skills, consider using these steps to add depth through shading. I suggest using basic 2H pencil, black-colored marking pencil, waterbrush, and white gel pen.

1. Sketch the basic outline of a figure onto a journal page, using a 2H pencil. Pencils with a lead strength from 2H to 4B are good options **(fig. A)**.

2. Add shading with a black-colored marking pencil. Blend the shading with a waterbrush (or a wet paintbrush) **(fig. B)**.

3. Add highlights back in the drawing with a white gel pen **(fig. C)**.

fig. A

fig. B

fig. C

Alisa Burke
www.alisaburke.com

I consider journaling, or in my case sketching, to be my daily *creative workout*. The practice of working through a page or two every day keeps me *"warmed up"* and inspired to make art. The process of creating from start to finish is such an important way for me to *grow and develop* my creative skills, to work through things that make me get better as an artist. Over time, I've noticed that this daily ritual of sketching in my journal pages has made me *more disciplined* in making art.

WHEN I'M STUCK

To gain confidence in the journaling process, I recommend the following:

* *Be consistent.* Often, you don't associate lots of discipline with being creative, but a consistent commitment to create a page a day will pay off in other areas of your life.

* *Quiet your inner critic.* In my opinion, a journal should be the one place you are free to do whatever you want without thinking too much! Instead of being critical or trying to get things perfect, treat your pages as a place to do simple experiments and work through your ideas. This is your time and place to practice and to experience trial and error.

OPPOSITE AND LEFT

Never underestimate the power of a tiny little flower or leaf. Because once you make a tiny one, you can build upon it by adding many more layers of petals, dots in varying sizes, and different types of swirls. Before you know it, the entire page will beautifully blossom.

ABOVE

Sketching and painting objects that don't have much color, like these feathers, opens up opportunities to experiment with varying shades of gray, as well as how to add colors to the background to make the objects stand out.

Everyday Exploring

All of my pages are about exploring ideas, shapes, colors, and everyday things. I typically don't go into creating a page expecting an outcome or perfect finished product. Instead, I look to practice my sketching and watercolor skills and to explore ideas with color, pattern, and design. I often use images and things from my life as a place to start.

I start by sketching everything out with a pen and then go back in and fill my sketches with watercolors. I finish by adding details with a fine-tip black marker.

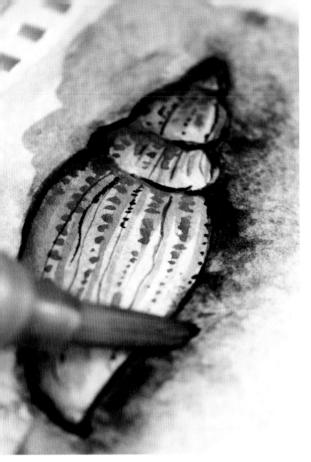

g. A

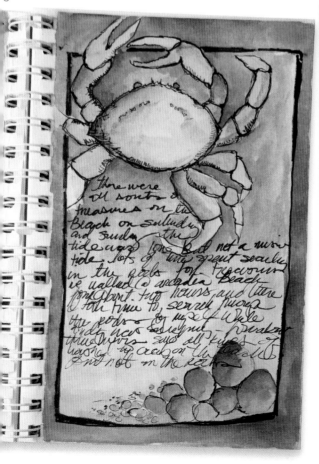

WHAT YOU'LL NEED

* Journal
* Pen
* Watercolors
* Paintbrush
* Waterbrush
* Fine-tip black marker

TECHNIQUE

1. Create a small drawing with a pen. Shown here are drawings of shells, but any object from your life will also work. Perhaps car keys, stones, or coins. Just look around to find your inspiration. Fill in the drawing with a wash of watercolor.

2. Add details with a tiny brush and dark saturated watercolor.

3. Add more details with a larger brush and saturated color. Let dry.

4. Fill in some lines and details as desired with a fine-tip black marker.

5. Add a wash of light watercolor around the edges of the image. This will make the image pop and add more overall interest and dimension (**fig. A**).

TIPS

* Laying down a wash of watercolor is a great way to fill in areas of space on a page.
* Use a paper towel to blot the surface of color. It will pull color away and add highlights.
* Add details to the surface by varying the thickness, size, and weight of the brushstrokes. Shown here are strokes made with a waterbrush. The effects can also be made with a regular paintbrush (**fig. B**).

fig. B

Tools for Creativity

As on all of my pages, I started by making the drawings with a pen and then filling in with watercolors. The added gray around all of the objects adds a nice depth to them.

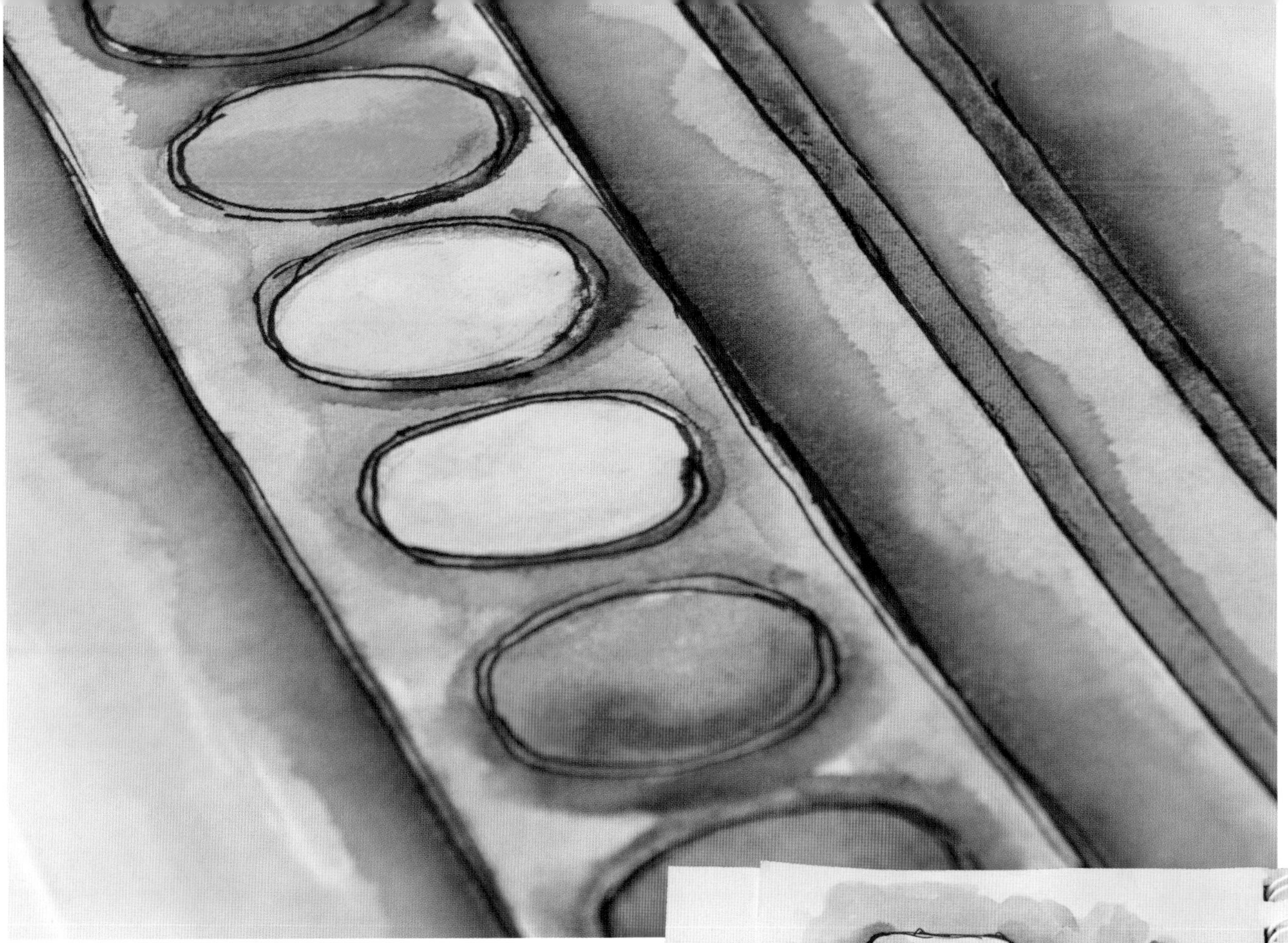

INSIGHT

Aside from my sketchbook,
there are just a few things
I need to create my pages:
watercolors, a paintbrush or
two, and some pens. Keeping
things simple in terms of tools
and materials allows me to
focus on the details of life.

Framing

After I draw and color my subject matter, I like to put a simple frame around it with a black marker. This allows the subject to look much more finished and allows for the non-framed area to be a natural space to do journaling.

INSIGHT

I love to wear boots and it was fun to draw and paint my favorite brown pair of boots that come up to my knees. To make the red outside the frame a bit softer, I added a wash of white before journaling.

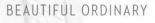

khaki
green

pea
green

Brown

terracotta

fall colours for dressing bright J Brown with my favorite pea green pea

Red

BEAUTIFUL ORDINARY

Since I mostly create pages full of sketches, I don't use prompts. But I do challenge myself to use things from my everyday life and routine. For instance, if I am cooking a colorful meal, I will draw and paint the food, then journal about it. Or if I take a trip to the beach, I will sketch all the treasures I find. And if I am wearing a certain outfit that inspires me, I will draw and paint my outfit!

Susanna Gordon

www.susannassketchbook.typepad.com

My art journals/sketchbooks are a *collection* of magazine *tear sheets*, written notes for projects, rough photographs, and *sketches* that I use for reference when creating my artwork. Back when I printed photographs in the darkroom, I took notes of all the *technical information* that I followed when creating a certain photograph or series of photographs. This would include the types and ratios of developers, archival photo paper stock, what filters were used and in which order, the length of exposures, etcetera. Those journals were *photographic cookbooks*. Nowadays, I shoot, process, and print my images digitally. Most of the technical notes are added onto the names of the digital files themselves. So, the journals have become more of a place where I can sort through ideas. There are certain *themes* that have *resurfaced* over the last ten years. One example is "water," be it a river, an ocean, or the act of bathing or swimming.

GETTING STARTED

I have a thing for good paper, so, when choosing a new sketchbook, I prefer books made with plain handmade papers. A problem can occur, though, when one of those books is so pretty that I don't want to mess up the first page by marking on it! So this is what I do to get over that:

✳ Buy an art journal/sketchbook that has a reasonable amount of pages, but not too many. I like to finish sketchbooks, so I never buy thick books.

✳ Have a sharp craft knife nearby to remove any pages that have been deemed "ruined." There's nothing wrong with removing a page or a section of a page that bothers you.

Having said that, there are plenty of pages in my sketchbooks where the ideas have been crossed out, with notes such as "Do this over" or "I don't like this." My sketchbooks are where I sort through ideas, not where I feature finished pieces of artwork, so I'm not worried whether a viewer will like every page. In fact, I think that artists, including myself, are interested in seeing how other artists work. What is his or her creative process? That includes ideas that work and ideas that don't work.

OPPOSITE

With just plain strips of masking tape, black and white photos can be simply and beautifully adhered inside a sketchbook ... to enjoy, to study, and to gather ideas for future shoots.

ABOVE

Journaling and sketching on plain lined paper or other scratch paper can happen when life is happening and the sketchbook is not nearby. These papers can easily integrate into the journal by tearing them out and attaching them to a journal page with tape.

LEFT

It is always interesting to see how a sketch evolves into a photograph, as the camera, model, and environment all mingle with the original vision for the photograph.

The Moth Collector

This project started with a simple skeleton lady doll I intended to create and donate for an online art auction with a "Day of the Dead" theme. However, a couple of personal obstacles that fell onto my path prevented her from being completed in time for the auction. Instead, my skeleton lady became a character for a story in my head.

The Moth Collector.

Bleeding from glue on previous page.
Will reprint.

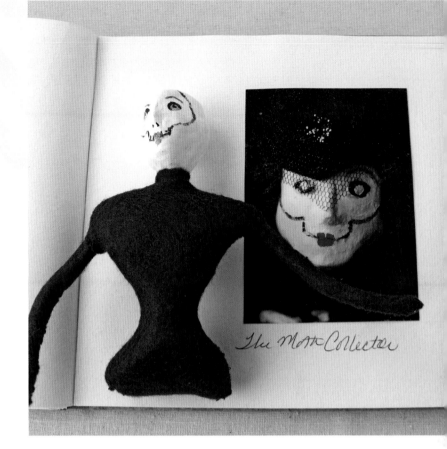

As I was making her, I thought of the summer and the thick woods near where I live, where my husband and I often go mountain biking. I thought of the insects and animals that come out at night when we humans are asleep in our beds. I thought of the gorgeous Alexander McQueen exhibit that I recently saw at The Met in New York, and of the late British designer's Victorian-inspired clothing line. Eventually, all of these ideas had me looking through old magazine images of Victorian-inspired clothing, and through the box of fabric remnants and ribbons that seem to follow me wherever we move.

I thought of Victorian butterfly collectors, particularly the women in their long-sleeved coats and long skirts, who traveled to exotic countries in search of butterflies. I imagined the spirit of one such woman searching for moths flitting through the dark woods.

The pages shown from my sketchbook document my journey and process related to the final creation of my project, "The Moth Collector."

The Moth Collector, Pages 3 and 4

The elements for page 3 were found and printed, or photographed and printed, at different times. Both photographs were taken during a visit to a butterfly arboretum. They were kept in a bag of miscellaneous images until I had the idea for "The Moth Collector."

For page 4, the original images of the moths were drawn on a separate piece of paper and given a wash of watercolor. Then that image was photocopied and pasted into this sketchbook. The black felt shape of the death's head moth was made from an enlarged photocopy of an image I found on the Internet. I then used the felt pattern to trace the shape onto a brown paper bag. From there, I built up the moth shape in papier-mâché and covered the entire piece in gloss varnish.

moth brooches!
Perfect on wool coats and cashmere sweaters!

INSIGHT

"The Moth Collector" is purely a whimsical creation. She is a creature from a story in my head—that of the spirit of a Victorian woman who wanders through the woods at night, capturing moths. The death's head moth has been used to symbolize death in mythology and in contemporary literature and films.

7 seconds
1 ½ filter
forté museum-weight warmtone fb paper.

Shown at the Chicana Humanities +
Arts Center, Denver, Colorado.
Nov 1-18, 2002

Day of the Dead, Page 1

I photographed my friend Laurie Maher wearing a vintage black dress with skeleton makeup on her face, jumping in shallow water along a beach. I printed the contact sheet (rows of film negatives printed onto photo paper) in the darkroom. I taped the contact sheet into the sketchbook and wrote notes onto the paper. On the following spread, I also added a larger print to the page with tape.

INSIGHT

Whenever I photograph a person, especially when they are moving or in a setting that has elements I cannot control, I find and hope that something unexpected will happen. It could be in the facial expression or pose of my subject, or the way the wind is blowing through fabric, or, as in this particular case, the patterns of the waves washing upon the shore.

As I wrote in the notes underneath the contact sheet, I wasn't satisfied with the images. I was so hard on myself back then, always reshooting and reshooting an idea. It's not a bad idea to have a lot of rough images to choose from, but in the end, I returned to this first contact sheet and chose the middle image for the final, good print.

I journal because it allows me to *express* my thoughts and ideas. Drawing and creating pages with visual elements also allows me to *explore different mediums* and to process ideas about future work. I love the *act of recording*. I love how it *connects me* to the moment or place I am in and how I can look back and reflect upon life lived and experience gained.

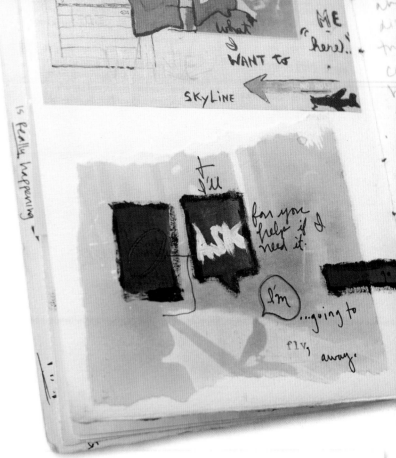

WHEN I'M STUCK

When I feel stuck with a page, I give myself a jump-start. One of my go-to ideas is to make a calendar or small squares of what happened on a given day. By reflecting on the events of a day, I find that I am more intentional about looking at my surroundings. My best pages emerge when I am paying full attention. Another of my favorite ideas, especially when I am on vacation, is to go somewhere alone with the pure intention of drawing and recording what I see.

OPPOSITE

On this colorful page, a large image of a woman fills much of the space. But because there are blocks of color painted on top of that image, it ends up being less intrusive and more of a layer that helps all of the other elements work together.

ABOVE

A page filled with handwritten text next to one filled with images can make a spread more visually compelling. Occasionally allowing color and sketching to spill over onto the handwritten text can also add interest.

LEFT

Making marks in wet paint or medium is a great way to add depth and texture. This area started with a layer of red acrylic paint that was allowed to dry, followed by a layer of white acrylic. While the white layer was still wet the word "Plan" was written into it using a dull pencil.

Sarah Atwater Bourne   87

Toner-Based Transfer

The keys to this technique are the colorless blender and the toner-based photocopies. You can purchase a colorless blender at any craft store that sells good-quality art markers. Other solvents also work for transferring toner-based photocopies but the colorless blender marker is the least toxic and least messy way of achieving a good result.

WHAT YOU'LL NEED

* Journal
* Black-and-white toner-based photocopies of images or text
* Colorless blender
* Wooden spoon or bone folder

TECHNIQUE

1. Place the toner-based copy right side down onto a journal page, so the toner touches the page.

2. Mark the entire image with the colorless blender from the wrong side of the toner-based copy. You will begin to see the image come through the back of the paper (**fig. A**). Note: Complete this step in a well-ventilated area, as the colorless blender emits toxic fumes.

3. On the back of the paper, rub the entire image with the back of a wooden spoon or a bone folder. Use consistent pressure and hold the paper firmly with your hands so the paper does not move around (**fig. B**).

4. Lift one corner of the toner-based copy gently off of the journal paper to reveal the fully transferred image.

5. Allow the page to air out for a minute before closing the journal shut or adding to the page.

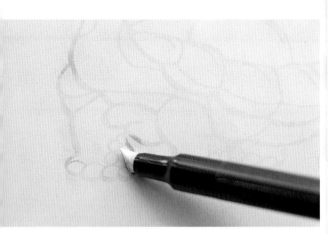

ig. A

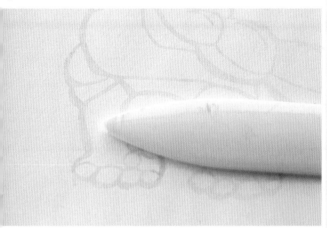

ig. B

The Plan, Scoville Journal, 2005

I cut squares and rectangles from magazines and an old postcard, then arranged them onto the spread and glued them down. I also added a piece of cheesecloth and then filled the empty spaces with rectangles and squares using acrylic paint. Once the page was dry I added contrasting colors of paint, which I wrote into using a dull pencil while they were still wet.

INSIGHT

This spread acted as a visual collection of thoughts about organizing and mapping spaces. These topics are of continued importance to me in my work and I often come back to this spread when I need inspiration. I love the combination of paint and handwritten text.

Asheville Journal, 2008

I prepared the exterior of the matchboxes with a combination of painting, collaging typewritten text, drawing, and layering photocopy transfers. Next, using the same combination of techniques, I cut and prepared papers that would fold and fit inside the boxes.

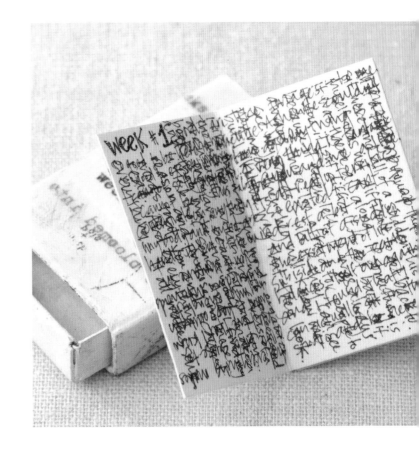

INSIGHT·

In the summer of 2008 I returned to Asheville, North Carolina, to rent a studio space at BookWorks (*www.ashevillebookworks.com*). Each week I wrote down thoughts on a small folio that fit inside an old matchbook. By the end of my trip, I had a new kind of journal that was both a record of my thoughts and a sculptural object. I enjoy branching out from the traditional book in order to utilize other ways of recording.

sunday march 18 2007

Mom is inside listening to the monks (do they call them that in Italy?) sing. I told her I could not be inside another church! So I have chosen to be outside to draw the olive trees.

We ate yogert in the car and walked a dirt path / drive to get to this church. It is beautifully overgrown... old, old olive trees surround me.

There are many people — but all seem to be doing their own thing. Boys and girls in uniforms?

So much wind in my face.

dried flowers!

olive leaves.

olive tree - sand in my face!

Olive Tree, Italy Journal, 2007

I first drew the trunk of the tree with a black ink pen and then used watercolors to fill it in. I also used the pen to doodle some branches and write the words. The flowers and leaves came from where I was sitting while journaling, which I pressed dry and attached to the page.

dried flowers!

007

...rks
...ing. I
...side
...walked
...urch.
...old
...t all seem

INSIGHT

I planned to draw the whole tree but ran out of time. Instead of continuing, I closed my journal. When I returned to our hotel room, I painted the trunk using watercolors and filled the remaining space with writing about my day.

Susan Shelley

The process of journaling has changed the way I think from day to day, particularly if I am journaling about a particular subject. The journal becomes like *a magnet* that *collects random ideas* and images that are generated initially by that subject. This collection of images, thoughts, and ideas affects me and at times alters the way I relate to the subject matter. There is also a *retrospective factor* to journaling, in that it often *ties together* my disconnected memories from the past. Journaling enriches my life and is more than simply sketching or recording an image. It extends, exponentially, my creative and imaginative life.

OPPOSITE

A beautiful and colorful photo takes center stage on this page. The photo becomes "framed" with small scraps of torn paper that are adhered and then outlined with a fine-tip black marker and some journaling.

LEFT

Chunky hand stitches were added to a piece of stenciled canvas before it was machine-stitched onto the journal page.

BELOW

A lovely image of green herbs was cut and stitched onto a piece of cheesecloth. These layers were adhered onto a book page that had been prepared with a layer of white gesso. Random strokes of watercolor were added to the outer edges of the cheesecloth.

NO RULES!

I say that there are no rules in art. In my opinion, trying to make art according to broad generalizations limits and stunts creativity. I like to create on a case-by-case basis. I always think to myself, "What do I want to say?" and then, "What methods am I going to use to say it?" There are times when you need to use simplicity so as not to cloud an idea that you want to get across. Other times you may feel quite emotional about something and want to throw in all the color, glitz, and razzmatazz that you can find. Remember: No rules!

Essence of Home

The background for this spread was completed in an old book that I decided to alter into a journal, months before everything else came together. I like preparing backgrounds in this manner and then allowing a memory, an occasion, or a found item to trigger the rest of the process.

Home 2020

Home is where my heart is and
my spirit finds peace and reple...
Long hours spent in repose on the ve...
observing the passing of time and
mulling over memories and where...
essence of all that means most co...
feed and nourish my creative s...
My best moments and my greatest...
are to be found here
Susan Marguerite Shelley

WHAT YOU'LL NEED

* Old book: 5½ x 8½ inches (14 x 21.6 cm)
* White gesso diluted with water (using a 3-to-1 gesso-to-water formula)
* Sponge brush
* Walnut ink solution in a mist bottle (see Walnut Ink on page 101)
* Sea salt crystals
* Mist bottle filled with water
* Paper towels
* Scissors
* Black paper scrap
* Decoupage glue
* Fabric paper (see How to Make Found Fabric Paper on page 102)
* String
* Photograph
* Burlap and fabric scraps
* Fine-tip black marker
* Cording

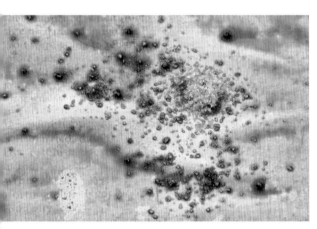

ig. A

ig. B

TECHNIQUE

1. Coat an entire spread with diluted gesso, using a sponge brush.

   Note: The reason I prefer working with diluted gesso is that it covers the page quicker and dries quicker than plain gesso. This gives you more control over how intense you want the coverage to be, since you can control the number of layers you put on the paper.

2. Mist walnut ink solution onto the entire gessoed spread.

3. To get a spotted effect, sprinkle sea salt crystals onto the wet walnut ink in desired areas **(fig. A)**. Once the walnut ink is completely dry, brush off the salt crystals with your hand.

4. Dry-brush the diluted gesso here and there to continue refining the aged, distressed, and faded look.

   Note: If at any time I feel I have added too much ink or gesso, I will mist the page with water and then dab it with paper towels. I never throw these paper towels away. I keep them in a separate box so that I can tear them up and use them, either for making Found Fabric Paper or in other layouts to add more textural interest.

5. To add a frame, cut black paper into your desired shape and adhere it to the page with decoupage glue. Cut fabric paper with a template; I used a bird, but any animal or simple shape would work. Adhere random scraps of string and machine-stitching to the cut-out fabric, and adhere it onto the black paper **(fig. B)**.

6. If you'd like to feature a photo, custom-fit a frame by cutting out the center portion of a burlap square. Adhere the photo onto a fabric scrap, and then adhere the burlap frame onto the photo. Attach the layers to the page with decoupage glue.

7. Use a fine-tip black marker to add details and journaling. Add cording or other ephemera with decoupage glue.

Autumn Sunrise

I collaged ephemera papers, adhering them with decoupage glue onto the spread to create the background. I moved the pieces around until I felt they suited the photos that I wanted to use. Once the background was created, I tore the edges of the pages. I sewed the borders of the photos with a sewing machine and attached them to the left side.

INSIGHT

Autumn is my favorite time of year, particularly as I have lupus and cannot go out in the hot sunshine. Therefore, I appreciate autumn and am usually up early to make the most of the days outside. I savor the sunrises and the sunsets before the chill of winter arrives. That year was particularly poignant for me as our nine-year-old granddaughter was battling leukemia and each sunrise held hope for another day in her life.

WALNUT INK

Walnut ink is made from the husk of walnuts. Some artisans make their own walnut ink by boiling walnuts and their husks in a large pot of water. Walnut ink is readily available at art supply stores either in liquid form or crystal form. The crystal form is used by diluting it with hot water.

HOW TO MAKE FOUND FABRIC PAPER

WHAT YOU'LL NEED

* Work surface covered with plastic
* Muslin, 8 x 10 inches (20.3 x 25.4 cm)
* Scraps of thin found papers (like stained paper towels, sewing pattern tissue, book pages)
* Decoupage glue diluted with water (using a 3-to-1 gesso-to-water formula)
* White tissue paper, 8 x 10 inches (20.3 x 25.4 cm)

TECHNIQUE

1. Place the muslin onto the prepared work surface.

2. Brush a scrap of thin found paper with diluted decoupage glue using a paintbrush, and place it onto the muslin. Repeat with other found paper scraps until the entire muslin is covered. It is okay for the scraps to extend beyond the edges of the muslin, which can be trimmed away later.

3. Paint the entire paper-covered muslin with another layer of diluted decoupage glue and then layer the entire piece with a large piece of white tissue paper.

4. Apply another layer of diluted glue on top of the white tissue paper. Allow the paper to dry for 24 hours.

Sunshine, Freedom, and a Little Flower

These two pages have a gessoed background and walnut ink sprayed with an atomizer. I love how the images of the roses and geranium add so much color and energy to the spread. I added some vintage lace and a bow I had kept with other bits and bobs over the years.

sunshine
freedom
and a little flo
Hans Christian
Anderson

INSIGHT

The pink roses were a delightful discovery in the garden of a house we had just moved into. And the blue geraniums are something I had brought from the garden of my former home. So this spread is all about something old and something new, with a quote that helps me reflect my happiness in my new garden.

Corey Moortgat

www.coreymoortgat.blogspot.com

I didn't become a full-blown journal artist until I got married and started having children. I am such a sentimental person; I needed a way to *document* my *memories* of special events and milestones. Over time, it has just become part of who I am, as a mother, and as an artist. My pieces may *not always* have actual written journaling on them, but they almost always have *personal meaning* and significance.

OPPOSITE

The imperfectly painted white lines couple well with the smudgy and "imperfect on purpose" journaling made with a graphite pencil.

LEFT

Scallops made with a white gel pen elevate the cut illustration and piece of journaled paper without too much effort. The scallops can also evolve with the addition of paints and pens.

BELOW

Once a photo or illustration is cut into a certain shape and adhered to a page, it can influence how the rest of the page develops and ultimately balances out.

WHEN I'M STUCK

If you feel overwhelmed getting started with a blank book that is filled with white pages, do what I do, which is to start with an old book that is filled with printed pages. You can gesso the pages or paint colored washes on the pages. Just having that text already there, and then putting a wash of something onto those pages, helps me break that initial barrier. I also almost always begin my process with a piece of ephemera, like a photo or vintage illustration or collage element. Having even just one image means that you have a starting point from which to work and build upon.

Reverse Silhouettes

As mentioned, I almost always begin my process with a piece of ephemera. For this spread, I used an image and an illustration that work very well together because they are both of girls in pigtails. This reverse silhouette technique is wonderful when using images and illustrations that complement one another.

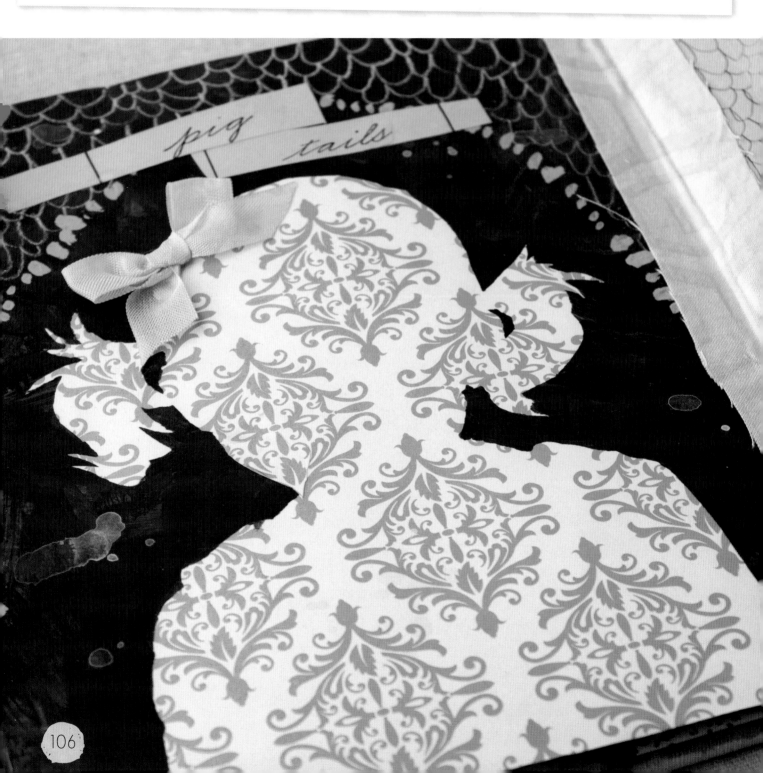

WHAT YOU'LL NEED

* ✳ Old book
* ✳ Photograph of a child
* ✳ Vintage illustration of a child
* ✳ Small detail scissors
* ✳ Acrylic paint in coordinating colors
* ✳ Paintbrush
* ✳ Adhesive
* ✳ Assorted paper ephemera
* ✳ Pencil
* ✳ White-colored pencil or charcoal pencil
* ✳ Coordinating shades of acrylic paint in greens and pinks

TECHNIQUE

1. Select an image and a vintage illustration that share a common theme. For this spread, I selected an image of my daughter in pigtails and a vintage illustration of a little girl also in pigtails. Be sure to select an image with shapes that can translate nicely into a silhouette.

2. Cut the outline of the image with the scissors, paying close attention to details like stray hairs.

3. Place the cutout image onto decorative paper. Hold the image in place with your hand and then apply dark paint around the cutout in a dabbing motion, as you would if using a stencil. Be sure to brush the paint away from the image so that no drips go underneath the image.

4. Continue painting the rest of the decorative paper and pull the photo up to reveal the reverse silhouette.

5. Paint the opposite side of the spread and allow the spread to dry.

6. Adhere the vintage illustration along with additional pieces of ephemera. Draw a simple scale motif on the painted page, using a pencil. Draw the same motif on the reverse silhouette page with a white pencil.

7. Add dabs of paint in your choice of colors on both pages, and paint stripes in shades of various colors on the painted page. Allow all the paint to dry.

8. Add journaling to the stripes with pencils. I used white-colored and charcoal pencils.

Mother Held the Baby

There is really no formula for creating organic shapes. They are shapes that just naturally flow, inspired by images and illustrations. For this spread, I used a photo and illustration where reading is the common thread. I cut the photo and illustration so that both would have a softer feel. These shapes inspired the organic shapes that I painted and collaged in repetition.

June 16, 2008
You just adore books these days, and you are so persistant about me reading them to you. Any time I'm on the floor, you come over and plop down in my lap with a book!

Mother held the baby in her lap.
(laps)

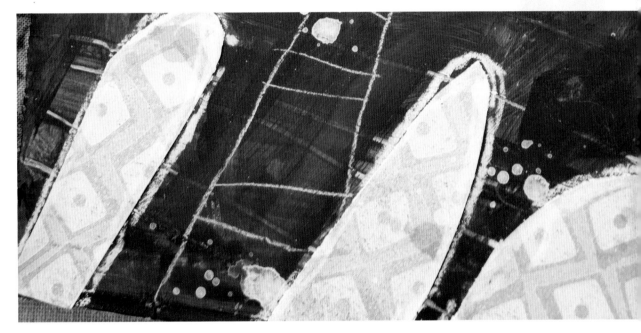

INSIGHT

I like the back-and-forth movement of these pages, which has something to do with the fact that I tend to make shapes that lean a little bit. On these pages, I experimented with objects leaning in both directions, which adds to the energy and interest of the spread.

You started playing with toys

You tried your first food – rice cereal

You discovered you have feet

Four Months

I started by collecting vintage illustrations that would complement photos of my child in her varying stages of development. I first adhered the images and illustrations, then I painted around those elements with bright shades of acrylic paint. Once dry I went back and applied gray paint over the first painted colors, leaving some of the page unpainted, to allow the colors to show through.

INSIGHT

I am frequently asked how I get a chalky effect with the paints I use on my journal pages. Honestly, the answer is that I just use the inexpensive craft paints that come in small plastic bottles. The only thing I pay attention to is whether the bottle is labeled "transparent" or "opaque." I tend to not like the transparent ones. The paint goes straight from the bottle onto my journal pages. Perhaps the chalky effect is due to the fact that I am painting on book pages for the most part, which is a drier surface than other types of paper or substrates.

Kathrin Jebsen-Marwedel

www.flickr.com/photos/98657307@N00/

In the past, I kept a written diary, but anytime I noticed that there wasn't enough room to write down all my thoughts and everyday occurrences, *I began to draw* the most important happenings of every day and *write only a few words*. The upside to this is that when I browse through my journals, *I can remember at a glance* what I did each day on nearly every page. I love to be creative, to draw and paint, and I love to preserve my thoughts and experiences in drawings.

ILLUSTRATED DIARY

In 2005, I discovered Flickr and noticed that there are so many other people who use their journals as an illustrated diary. For a few months I was just an observer and was so amazed with all those drawings and different styles. The best part was to see that people have fun, and it isn't their priority to show only absolutely perfect drawings. So I dared to load up some of my drawings; I wanted to be not only a profiteer of all those ideas, but also a contributor.

OPPOSITE

One of the benefits of using small rubber stamps is that they can be stamped multiple times and in varying directions, quickly and easily.

ABOVE

Sometimes, limiting your color palette to just two or three colors can be a great way to create a somber and sophisticated mood.

LEFT

Aerial views are challenging to sketch. But sometimes, rather than laboring over a process to create a realistic aerial view, it's fun (and freeing) to distort and exaggerate the view.

Coloring Your Style

No matter how much you try, you won't be able to draw someone else's style exactly. It's nice to get ideas from other artists, but keep in mind that you will draw the way you draw. Because that's your style. So rather than telling you how to draw, I'd like to share with you how I fill in my drawings with color. This is my process.

fig. A

WHAT YOU'LL NEED

* Journal
* Mechanical pencil
* Very soft non-wax-based colored pencils
* Black waterproof fine-tip pen
* Watercolors
* Felt markers in different colors
* Paintbrush
* Calligraphy pen with white waterproof calligraphy ink (or white gel pen)
* Letter stamps and black inkpad
* Fine-tip marker

TECHNIQUE

1   Create a sketch of people or things in a journal, using an ordinary mechanical pencil.

2   Trace parts of the sketch that you want to emphasize with a black waterproof pen **(fig. A)**.

3   Add watercolors to the sketch, and let dry **(fig. B)**.

4   Add contrast with felt markers. Blend the lines between the watercolors and pens with a paintbrush loaded with a bit of water.

5   Add details with a calligraphy pen and white waterproof ink or a white gel pen.

6   Add journaling with letter stamps and a black inkpad, as well as a fine-tip marker.

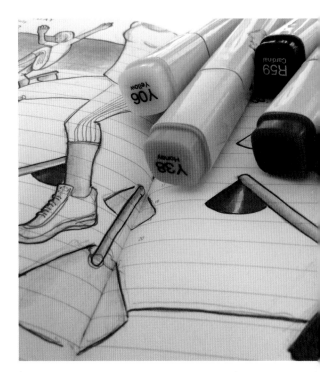

fig. B

Kathrin Jebsen-Marwedel   115

Candy Fish

For my drawing I used very soft non-wax-based colored pencils and a fine-tip black ink pen. The weather stamp in the left corner is my own design. In the original stamp there are only three raindrops, but it was such a rainy day that I added some more. I also used a date stamper; I bought it in Greece, which is why it has Cyrillic letters.

FRIDAY
February
4

11 °C

05 ΦEB. 2011 ROBERT FÄHRT
NACHMITTAGS ZUM KICKERTURNIER IN DIE
MEIEREI; VORMITTAGS
HOLTENAUER-
BUMMEL.

SATURDAY
February
5

Hermann Hinrichs
Bonbonkocherei
Frau-Clara-Straße 22

04 ΦEB. 2011 **jack's kitchen** soulfood für kiel

NEU IN KIEL AM WESTRING. GUTE EINRICHTUNG; SPEISE-
KARTE PIZZA, PASTA, SALAT. ICH PROBIERE DEN SALAT —
KANN MAN BESSER MACHEN; HÄLT VERGLEICHEN IN DER
PREISKATEGORIE NICHT STAND. VAPIANO IST BESSER, SUBROSA
SOWIESO. ABER DEN SALAT TOPPT SO SCHNELL AUCH KEINER.
ROBERTS PIZZA IST OK. INSGESAMT: GUTER LADEN, MITTEL-
MÄSSIGE KÜCHE, PREISE GUT.

06 ΦEB. 2011 SONNTAG: VERKAUFSOFFENER SO. IN
ECKERNFÖRDE. ZUFÄLLIG ENTDECKEN WIR DIE BONBON
KOCHEREI, IN DER EINE SEHR NETTE VORFÜHRUNG STATT
FINDET. JETZT WEISS ICH, WIE MAN BONBONS MACHT!

week 5

INSIGHT

This spread was created after visiting a candy manufacturer where their process of making candy became a fun performance of sorts for the onlookers. For this particular demonstration, they made fish candies in the colors of the federal state where I live, in Schleswig Holstein, Germany.

STOP THE RUMINATION

Though it may sound simple, I really believe that the most effective advice I can give to anyone about overcoming mental blocks to journaling is to just do it! Buy a sketchbook or a journal and just do it. Begin to draw and make a mark. Stop the rumination, stop all the doubting, and have fun! Because believe me: your drawings will become good if you have fun doing them.

06 ФЕВ. 2011 SONNTAG: VERKAUFS
ECKERNFÖRDE. ZUFÄLLIG ENTDECKEN
KOCHEREI, IN DER EINE SEHR NETTE
FINDET. JETZT WEISS ICH, WIE MAN

Bruce Kremer

www.bkremer.com

I journal as a way to keep a visual diary. Journaling is a tool to record my thoughts, activities, and movements in visual form. I use a journal to *chronicle my life occurrences* and the world around me at a specific moment, while cataloguing objects I find worthy and noting observations *I deem special*. My journal is *a stew* of notations.

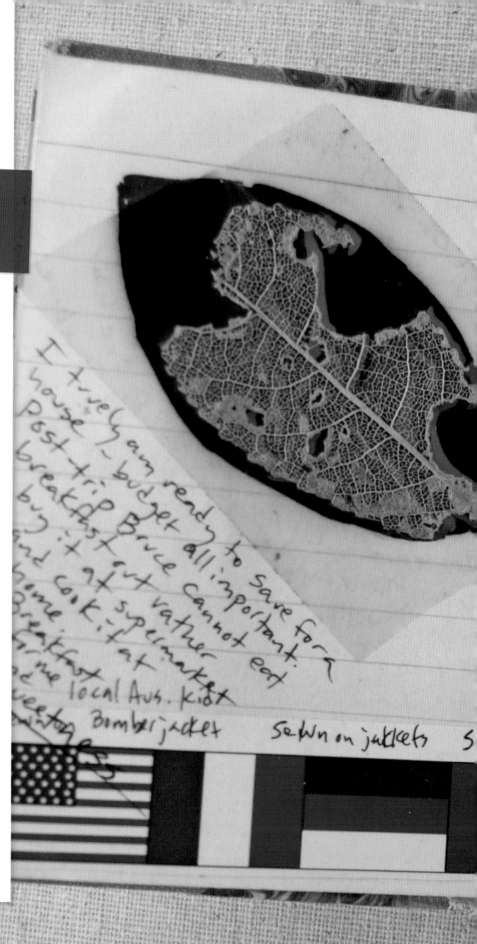

MY MUST-HAVES

Mentally, I must be in the right mindset to look for and collect objects and information around me, to have my journal close at hand, and to remember to take photographs. Physically, I need to have spray adhesive, an HB pencil, colored grease pencils, and 2-inch (5.08 cm) wide clear tape.

OPPOSITE

Practically anything can be secured into a journal with a bit of wide clear tape. When the object is organic, like this leaf, the appearance changes over time, which can be very cool.

ABOVE

A Wood Pigeon's feather, found in Australia, is one of several things recorded (with the aid of clear wide tape) within a smaller travel journal. This journal was filled during a six-month trip around the world in the early 1990s.

RIGHT

At this point, I've filled about 30+ of these journals. Every single page in every single book.

My Process

Many journal artists write passages of their feelings in the moment. My entries are largely visual without much access to my inner thoughts. I want to write more, but don't see it happening.

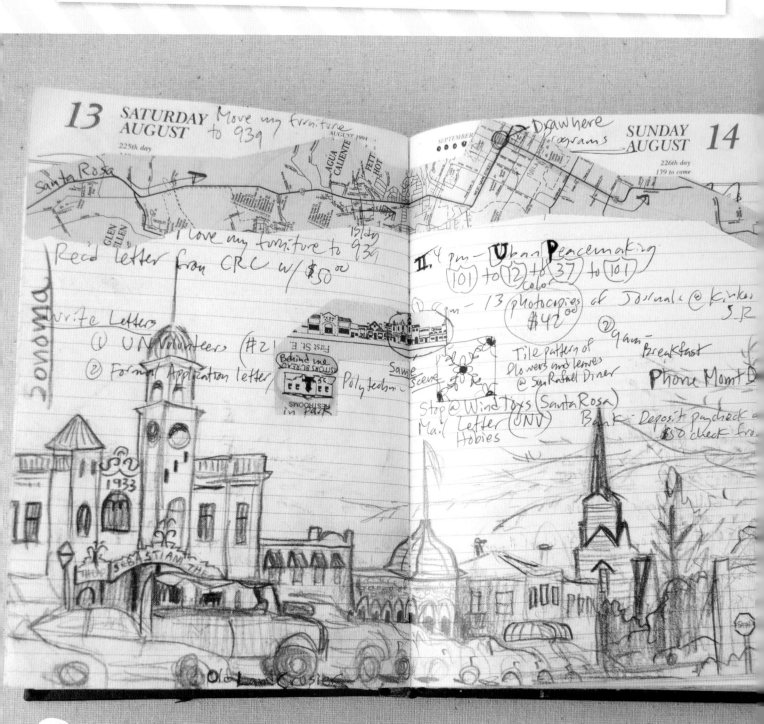

I am drawn to layering and filling space, even if it's just doodles. I need separate address and calendar books, in addition to the cluttered daily journal, to separate important information that might be needed in the future. Otherwise, it will be lost in the collaged chaos.

I have tried many things to keep the process going without interruption. I finally decided that a dated journal (daily planner) is imperative to keep me motivated. The notion of a blank page being revealed, if I lag, keeps me going and searching for materials for that page. Life presents interruptions, thus journal stoppages, but I often go back to the blank pages with "random" entries.

Since I use a daily planner for journaling, I have one completed book for each year since I began in the early 1980s. I also keep additional sketchbooks, large and small. When I take extended trips, I usually start a book just for the journey. I am committed to this medium forever. It is a part of me now.

July 10-11

Here is a spread that documents two of my days from 1999. I sketched the house belonging to my friend, Anne. I used watercolors to bring the sketch to life.

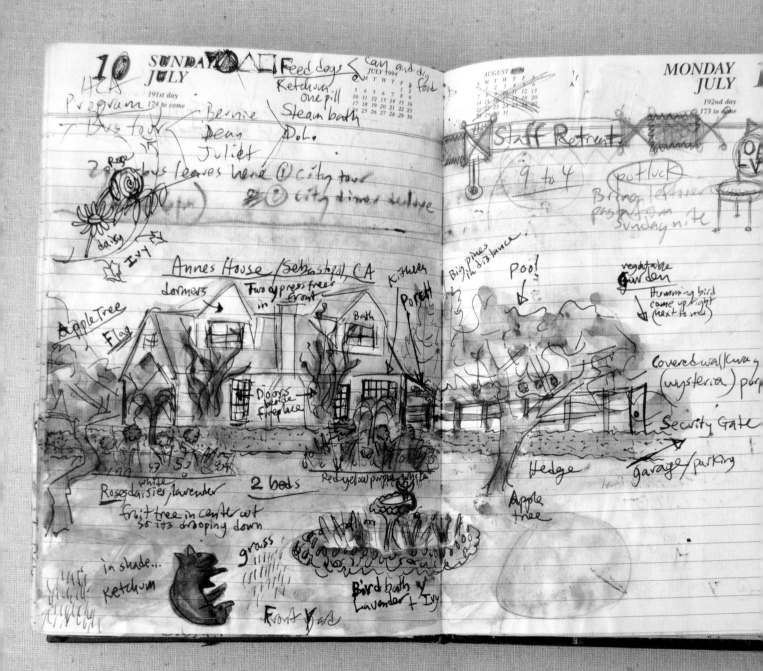

Within the sketch, handwritten notations read: "dormers", "Two cypress trees in front", "Porch", "Bath", "Doors beside fireplace", "2 beds", "Red yellow purple white", "white daisies / lavender", "it tree in center cut drooping down", "grass", "Bird bath"

GRATIFYING FEEDBACK

For many, many years, nobody saw my books except family and friends. It is not important for me that the books have viewers, as opposed to my other artwork, such as painting, drawing, and photography. Though I must admit, the reaction to my journals has been the most gratifying feedback I have received, more than from the other works.

INSIGHT

As much as I enjoyed working diligently on the details of the sketch and coloring, I also like that I allowed space for notations of the days to have a place on these pages. I like that no drawing is so precious that I can't have it share space with my ordinary chaos.

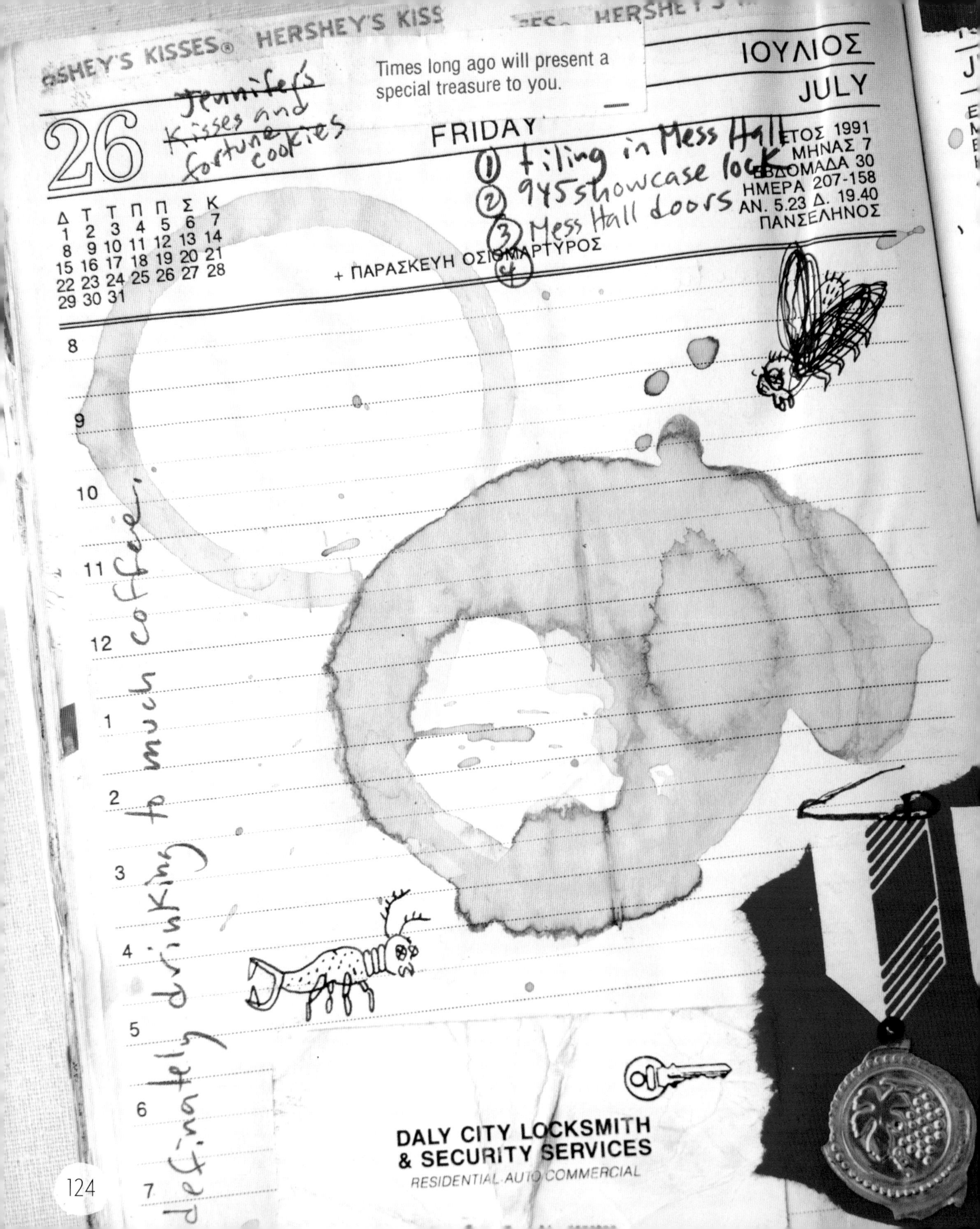

HERSHEY'S KISSES® HERSHEY'S KISS
Times long ago will present a special treasure to you.
ΙΟΥΛΙΟΣ
JULY
26
Jennifer's
Kisses and
fortune cookies
FRIDAY
ΕΤΟΣ 1991
ΜΗΝΑΣ 7
ΕΒΔΟΜΑΔΑ 30
ΗΜΕΡΑ 207-158
ΑΝ. 5.23 Δ. 19.40
ΠΑΝΣΕΛΗΝΟΣ
① filing in Mess Hall
② 945 showcase lock
③ Mess Hall doors
④
Δ Τ Τ Π Π Σ Κ
1 2 3 4 5 6 7
8 9 10 11 12 13 14
15 16 17 18 19 20 21
22 23 24 25 26 27 28
29 30 31
+ ΠΑΡΑΣΚΕΥΗ ΟΣΙΟΜΑΡΤΥΡΟΣ
8
9
10
11
12
1
2
3
4
5
6
7
definitely drinking to much coffee.
DALY CITY LOCKSMITH
& SECURITY SERVICES
RESIDENTIAL·AUTO·COMMERCIAL

July 26–27

Is there anything more perfect than the imperfect coffee stain? And once your page is stained, there's nowhere else but up for it to go.

INSIGHT

The rules of composition for these pages is that there are no rules. It's stream of consciousness. It's nonsense. It's notes. It's doodles of bugs. It's a feather I found, a letter I received, a locksmith I called.

Roben-Marie Smith

www.robenmarie.com

I was inspired to begin journaling by viewing the work of other journalers, and I realized I wanted to *offer inspiration* to others as well. At first, I was intimidated about putting my journal pages out there, but I feel differently now. *I share* my pages through my blog and Flickr, and I was also asked to share my work during an exhibit at a local gallery a couple of years ago. It was *a little scary*, but also *rewarding*, to watch as people pored over the pages of my journals and asked me questions and expressed interest in learning how to create their own.

SURE-FIRE PROMPTS

No matter how much journaling experience a person has, there are always instances when ideas and prompts are needed to get you started. If I need a boost to get me going, I find that making a list helps. Here are some ideas that work for me:

* Five things I need to do today.

* Five things I want to change about myself.

* Five things that make me happy.

In addition to lists, I also like to clip words from books and use them as jumping-off points. Also, if I'm at a loss for what to write on a page, I love simply writing lyrics from a favorite song.

OPPOSITE

If you don't know where on a painted page you should add journaling, consider adhering strips of lined or ledger paper to the page. These small strips can be very inviting for just a touch of easy-breezy journaling .

ABOVE

Back-and-forth free-motion stitching made right smack into the middle of a heart shape can transform a mood from sweet to edgy.

LEFT

Stencils, bubble wrap, and lids are wonderful mark-making tools. This page includes assorted stencil marks made with spray paint, lots of dots made with acrylic paint and bubble wrap, and random circles made with acrylic paints and the lid of a jar.

Inky Paper Backgrounds

To make inky paper, the most important thing is to not think about it. Simply place newsprint paper, scraps of actual newspaper, paper towels, or other scrap papers onto your work surface. As you are painting, splattering, and spritzing the project you are working on, the papers on your work surface will automatically get all inky and messy during the process. This is what I call "inky paper"—a wonderful element that you can use to create fabulous backgrounds in your journal pages. I don't like to waste paper or ink, and the newsprint has a nice feel to it once it dries. Inky papers allow truly random colors and images to be part of the journal page.

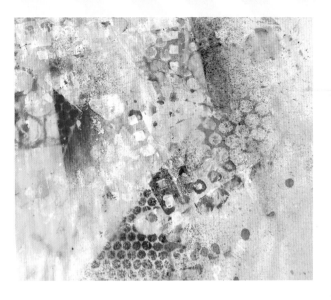

WHAT YOU'LL NEED

* Inky newsprint paper, slightly larger than the journal page
* Base journal page
* PVA glue (see Why PVA? on page 133)
* Foam brush
* Brayer
* Inky newsprint paper scraps
* Heavyweight premium dry wax paper
* White gesso

TECHNIQUE

1. Adhere inky newsprint paper onto a base journal page, using PVA glue and a foam brush.

2. Brayer the layers to smooth out all air bubbles. Trim off excess newsprint paper.

3. Layer inky newspaper scraps to the adhered inky newsprint paper, again using the PVA glue **(fig. A)**.

4. Paint random shapes onto dry wax paper with white gesso. Once dry, tear the dry wax paper and adhere onto the newsprint paper with PVA glue **(fig. B)**.

5. Use this inky paper background page to add additional collage work and journaling to complete the page.

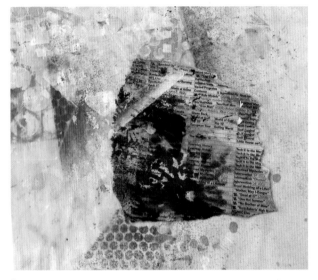

fig. A

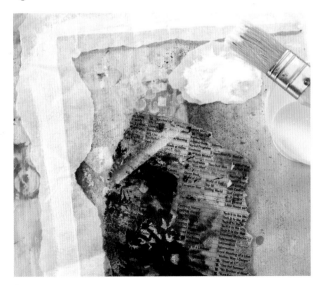

fig. B

Roben-Marie Smith 129

Stitched Blossoms

At first, machine stitching was something I used to attach items to a journal page, but then I realized how much I like the messy feel and texture it provides. I now use it much more as a design element. The chunky hand-embroidery stitches couple well with the machine stitches.

WHAT YOU'LL NEED

* Base journal page
* White gesso
* Palette knife
* Paintbrush
* Assorted shades of Glimmer Mist tints
* Spray bottle with water
* Paper circles
* Fabric scraps cut or torn into strips
* Sewing machine with black sewing thread
* PVA glue
* Small brush
* Hand-sewing needle
* Embroidery floss in assorted colors

fig. A

fig. B

TECHNIQUE

1. Prepare a base journal page by coloring it with any desired method. To create a background like the one shown here **(fig. A)**:
   * Apply white gesso to the page with a palette knife. Allow it to be very thick in some areas so you can "write" into the wet gesso with the pointed end of a paintbrush. Allow the page to dry.
   * Spray the page with a variety of Glimmer Mist tints. Glimmer Mist is a water-based product that contains fine mica powder. It can be spritzed onto paper to add a colorful and sparkly effect. Spritz a little water here and there and tip the page to merge some of the colors together. Allow the page to dry completely before moving to the next step.

2. Machine-stitch strips of fabric onto the page with black thread. Use messy and uneven stitches and allow the thread tails to remain long and untrimmed.

3. Adhere paper circles to the tops of the fabric strips with PVA glue.

4. Sew the "flower tops" to the paper circles using embroidery floss and a hand-sewing needle. Use a variety of embroidery stitches, exaggerating and modifying some as desired **(fig. B)**.

Jelly Beans are Colorful!

Inky newspaper (see page 129) was adhered to the page with PVA glue (see Why PVA? on opposite page). The brown bag was stitched to the page to create a pocket. A small scrap of paper was used to create a tag to be inserted into the pocket. Inky paper scraps were stapled randomly to the page, followed by doodles with a black marker and oil pastels. Masking tape, collage papers, and a sticker were added to the page. The white circle marks were made by applying white gesso to the bottom of a round paint cup and stamping it onto the page several times.

I remembered that...

Jelly beans are Colorful

and pockets are for Notes!

SEPTEMBER 16

REUSE OR RECYCLE THIS BAG

SALE PRICE $1

INSIGHT

The challenge for this page was to create a pocket. I loved the brown bag because of the "recycle" message printed on it. The inky paper I added was the perfect complement to the plain brown bag. Bottom line: Everything is fair game in an art journal—even brown bags!

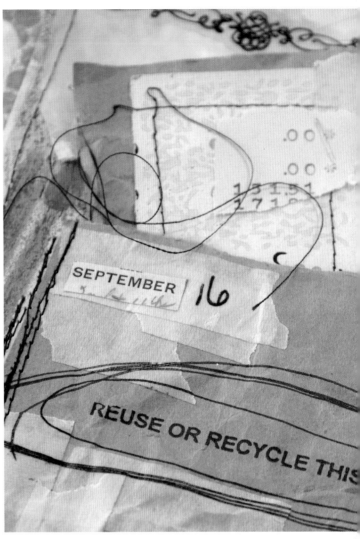

WHY PVA?

I have tried a lot of different glues and have found PVA to be versatile and consistent. I use a glue stick when I'm doing work quickly and with small pieces, but I like PVA for larger pieces of paper. The consistency is not too thick, nor is it too watery. It can be watered down if necessary and it still works great. I started using PVA when I was doing a lot of book binding and found it doesn't curl the paper as much as other glues. I like it and have continued to use it in my art journals.

Zom Osborne

www.pinchmetoseeifyouaredreaming.blogspot.com

I was a full-time artist for 19 years before I started art journaling. My journals are a **complement** to my studio practice. My paintings are detailed and meticulous, and it is a relief to splash and play in my art journal. It provides a kind of *counterbalance*. It helps to counteract my habit of perfectionism. Art journaling makes me a *better artist*.

TAKE A BREAK

I think journaling is a good remedy for conquering creative fear. One reason for this is you don't have to show anyone. It isn't like pulling out a canvas that just begs by its very form to be hung on a wall. An art journal is a book. It can easily be kept private. Another reason is because there are so many pages in a journal. You can start a bunch of pages at once, and if one isn't going well, you can flip to the next spread and then the next. You can decide to take a break from a spread for as long as you like, and then return to it later, with new and fresh ideas about what to do next.

OPPOSITE

The background for this page was created with the gesso resist method (page 137). The horizontal spike pattern made by the gesso is repeated in the vertical spikes of the girl's hair, balancing the page and adding movement.

ABOVE

Journaling does not have to be done with one pen, nor in one direction. By using different-colored pens and changing directions, the writing can become an additional design element.

LEFT

Doodles and drawings can be photocopied and used as collage elements. They can even be printed in a different size or painted with new colors to create transformed images. This is a great way to extend the life of the doodles and drawings and to use the mood of the image as a prompt for journaling.

Gesso Resist

Flowers and leaves are some of my favorite elements to use with this technique, but you can use practically anything to create a gesso resist on your journal pages. It's a fun and easy way to create depth, texture, and interest on background pages in preparation for journaling.

WHAT YOU'LL NEED

* Journal
* White gesso
* Flowers and leaves
* Paintbrush
* Coordinating colors of acrylic paint (optional)

fig. A

fig. B

TECHNIQUE

1. Gather items from nature or anything with a unique shape. I used leaves and flowers, but you can use whatever you can find. Gently paint your items with white gesso, using a paintbrush.

2. While the gesso is still wet, gently press the items onto the journal spread. (It is important that the paper is not gessoed beforehand.) Allow the gesso to dry (**fig. A**).

3. Place small dots of acrylic paint (desired color) onto the spread. Quickly spread the dots of paint all over the spread with a wet paintbrush until the entire spread is covered with the paint. You will notice that the areas with the gesso resist the paint, and the marks made with the gesso remain. Allow the paint to dry (**fig. B**).

4. To add more complexity of color, add a second shade of contrasting acrylic paint to the center of each page and spread with a paintbrush.

Under Collage

Under collage is basically what it sounds like. Instead of collaging over your background, the collage is the background. You can use pictures or writing for under collage. I prefer collaging from books that have special meaning for me, though I also love using a dictionary.

fig. A

fig. B

WHAT YOU'LL NEED

* Journal
* Pages from vintage books and dictionaries
* Ruler
* Matte gel medium
* Paintbrushes
* White gesso
* Acrylic paint in various colors
* Paper towel

TECHNIQUE

1. Place a ruler on top of a page in a vintage book and hold the ruler in place. Lift the page and tear. Repeat this process until you have enough torn book pages to be collaged onto the spread.

2. Collage the torn pieces of paper onto the spread with gel medium and a paintbrush, and allow to dry.

3. Apply a layer of white gesso over the entire spread with a paintbrush. Do not worry if you miss some spots, because ungessoed spots take the paint in the next step differently, which is an interesting effect. Allow the gesso to dry **(fig. A)**.

4. Apply a layer of acrylic paint over the spread with a paintbrush. Use a paper towel to wipe some of the paint off **(fig. B)**.

5. Repeat step 4 with additional shades of acrylic paints to build up color and texture until you are satisfied. Allow each layer to dry before adding the next layer.

Lucy Story

I stamped the background with gesso on this spread. Once dry, I added a thin layer of yellow paint, then wiped some of the paint off with a paper towel. Once that was dry, I taped off the border with masking tape, applied cobalt blue paint, then wiped that off. I used a photocopy of one of my sketched figures of a girl and collaged it (along with additional paper elements) onto the spread. I used a variety of gel pens to do the journaling.

Strangely I had a dream last night that I remembered while hearing this story...

Lucy Story:

of Lucy the chimp, kidnapped at 2 days and raised by a scientist as his wife (that's as their daughter. In 1977, they took her to Gambia to be released in the wild (Lucy was 11 or 12 years old). A young woman who cared for Lucy went as well and stayed behind to help her. She ended up taking the 'orphaned' chimps to an island and she lived in a cage in an attempt to separate from them, so they would learn to forage. (Janis ed Carter)

Alex the Dog Boy 2001 found in Talcahuano Chile Traian Caldarar 2002, Romania 3 years with wild dogs Ivan Mishukov 1998, Russia Dog Boy by Eva Hornung

It is too big... I must have been very big... I thought.

something very large & dark brown was

3 APR 2010

This journal is filled to the last page with back- grounds and I am thinking of the next journal. I have

1. I art

2. I be

3. I

INSIGHT

This page was created spontaneously over a week. I wasn't sure how to cut out the ends of the girl's hair. I didn't want to cut them off because I liked the blue tips, so I left some of the paper around the curls. I like the juxtaposition of the fish and the girl.

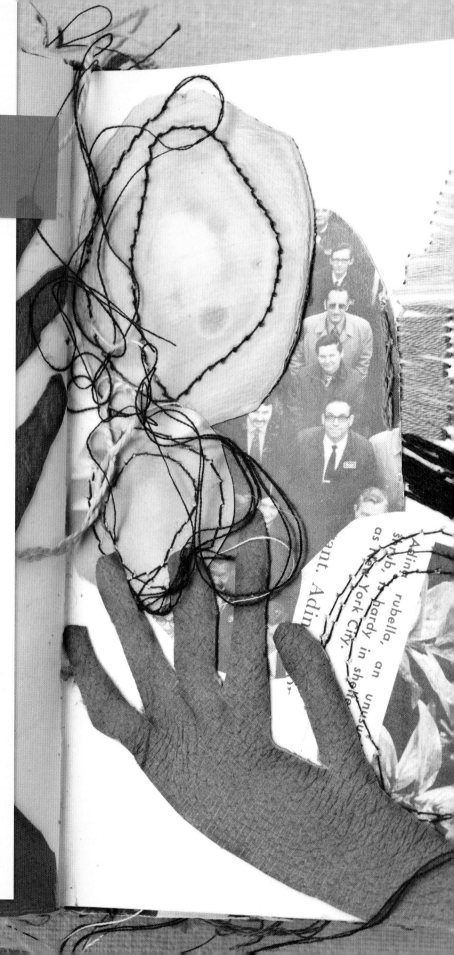

Alison Worman

www.alisonworman.com

The process of journaling for me is *quick and innate*. While working, I usually study the immediate relationships and conversations between my materials and myself. There is also something fascinating in the way that in a book, the back of one page is the front of another.

There is something about the structure of the sketchbook itself; it is *ongoing, always changing*. Through following my instincts and watching the relationships and connections that occur in my sketchbooks, I begin to create a *never-ending* study and *dialogue* that will always be important for me as an artist.

WITH A MARK

My high school art teacher persuaded us all to start our work with a mark, and I sometimes still work in this manner today. Starting with a mark can give you something to immediately work off of. Whether you cover it up or enhance it, you have given yourself some sort of ground, a jumping-off point for the rest of the page.

OPPOSITE

Laying down and layering images and elements quickly and without over-thinking things is what this spread represents. In the absence of precision, spontaneous and unexpected interest emerges.

ABOVE

The lines and angles from just a snippet of a magazine gets laid down, which inspires new lines sketched and stitched in different directions to be added.

LEFT

An effective method in visual journaling is to repeat what works. What works on this page is not only the repeating circles, but also the small pink pods and the tiny black lines.

The Give and Take

First I found the photo of a woman's hand while browsing through an old magazine. I immediately knew I wanted to use it, but felt it needed a counterpart. So I searched for a male hand to go along with it. After finding the right match, I placed the hands on the page. Then I needed some ground for the rest of the page so I added the peach fabric. I thought the color would accent the hands nicely. Lastly, I added the mesh to add more texture and make the page more dynamic.

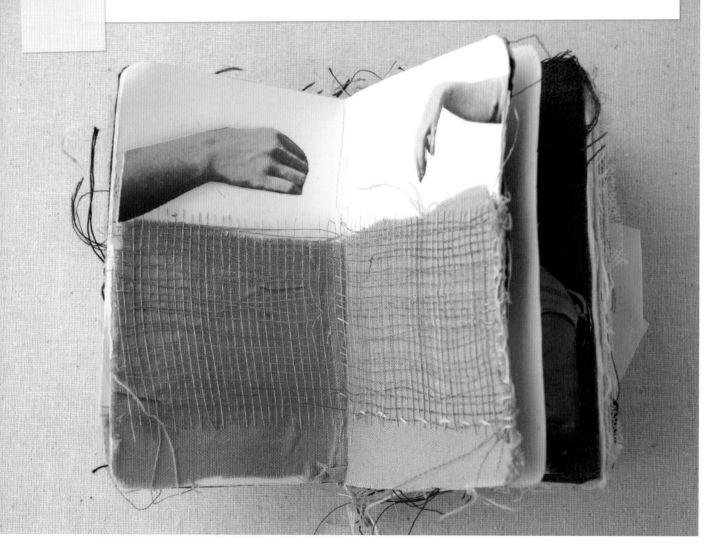

INSIGHT

For me, the hands symbolize the gesture of relationships, the give and take of it all. This is one of my favorite pages because it portrays a theme that I try to express frequently throughout my art in a very simple manner. I think finding the right magazine clippings for the hands was a rewarding search.

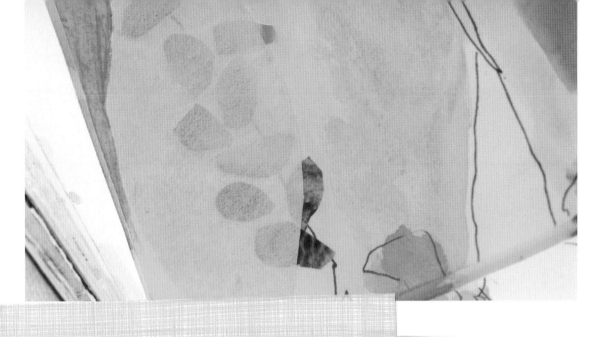

These Legs

I drew the image of the legs, then colored them with watercolor. Then I found an old photo I had taken, which had textures I liked. I cut this up into the little circle pieces and glued them down. I wanted them to be sort of hidden, so I covered them with the yellow tracing paper. The stitching in this piece is actually from the next page, but it just so happened to work with the other shapes on the page.

INSIGHT

This was more of a personal piece, reflecting body image. It was a good experience in watercolor for me, a technique I use only once in a while.

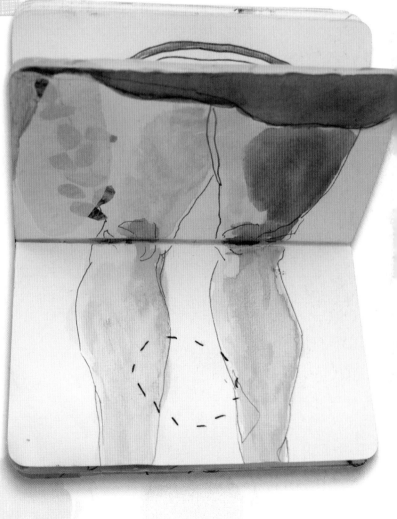

ALISON'S MUST-HAVES

Since I'm generally working at a fast pace, one thing that I cannot work without is a glue stick. It's perfect for adhering things quickly and it's less messy than any other glues. There's no waiting time for things to dry. Of course the downside of this is that the adhesive is not always as strong as I'd like. Sometimes I even have to go back and touch up the pages with a more permanent fix once I'm finished.

Another must-have is a needle and thread. I generally keep a couple of pre-threaded needles in my sketchbooks, so one is always available. I often like to attach things with needle and thread, while I also use it for embellishing and line work.

Another recent must-have is old magazines or old gardening books. I have a collection that I always have present in my sketch-booking space. I like to keep them around for inspiration, and then I usually use the imagery/color/texture from these books as an element in my collages.

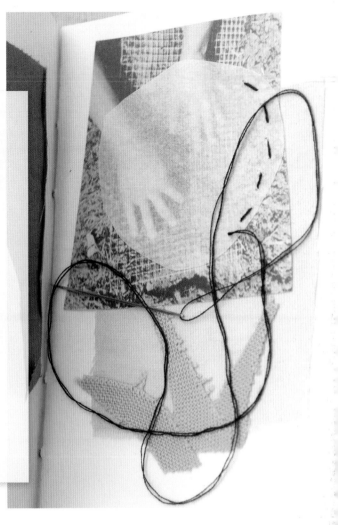

Little Windows

This page was a drawing I did long ago that I just never liked. I worked on it many times to try to get it to the right point, but just couldn't. I still wanted to know what the original drawing was, but at the same time I didn't want to see it in the same way anymore. I was working on a lot of cutout images for a different project when I got the idea to use the cutout windows for this piece. So that was the last thing I put down.

INSIGHT

I think this piece is important to me because I was able to work through and find a solution. The little cutouts let me see the color, texture, and line work that I enjoyed from the original drawing while transforming the main focus of the piece into the pattern of the cutouts.

Jeanette Sclar
www.despatchesfromlongears.blogspot.com

I journal to understand, to remember, to laugh, and to prove to myself that I was here and present. The very best part of life is the time spent *truly engaged* and interested. When I study and draw from nature, I see things I would miss if I just looked and admired. I know this to be literally true because I often *walk in the woods*, taking photos of wildflowers and making rough sketches with notes so I can *identify and paint* them. Nine times out of ten, I find that I have to return to the woods because I've failed to notice some critical identifying feature! I've come to *understand* that the camera is only as useful as the *mind* that chooses the shots. Who knew that the back side of a *flower* head often distinguishes it from its look-alike cousins? Or that a line of very *tiny hairs* along a stem do likewise?

INEVITABLE AUTHENTICITY

Authenticity is inevitable in journaling. I've taken classes and read books and tried lots of other people's techniques. The funny thing is that while I can come quite close to the results of others, my work is never quite like theirs. Sometimes that's because I lack their experience and sophistication, but my pages would not be authentic if they were a virtual clone of others. What I do take away from studying others' methods is a new vocabulary or a new set of tools. Over the long term, I find I incorporate some of these methods and disregard others, based entirely on what serves my feelings.

OPPOSITE

Images of eggs, whether sketched and painted or rubber stamped, provide ideal space for one- or two-word journaling.

ABOVE

Thorough observation of a nature subject, in this case a beautiful specimen of Queen Anne's Lace, is the most important part of sketching and watercoloring it within a journal page.

LEFT

For this page, the stitching around the edges needed to happen to secure attachments on the back side. With good planning, the stitching coordinates well in color and position with the watercolored flowers and journaling on the front side.

CLEMATIS JACKMANII
'SUPERBA'

CLEMATIS TEXENSIS
'DUTCHESS OF ALBANY'

ROSE
'NEW DAWN'

CLEMATIS
'BETTY BALFOUR'

CLEMATIS
FORGOTTEN

CLEMATIS
'EMPRESS OF INDIA'

CLEMATIS
'ROGUCHI'

LONICERA
LEMONADE-PINK

CLEMATIS
HYDRANGEA 'ENDLESS
SUMMER'

BETONY

Rabbit Garden Journal

I have gardened for many years with mixed success, due to the rabbit population here at Longears. Yes, I have named my tiny suburban plot after the crop I grow best. Each year, it seems I find a different method of garden record-keeping. The vegetable plot is the most important one to record since it's so small, and I don't want to repeat plantings of the same thing in consecutive years (which leads to disease and soil depletion). I'm all too aware that the rabbits will get a lot of it, so instead of calling this page my Vegetable Planting Plan, I call it the Rabbit Food Plan.

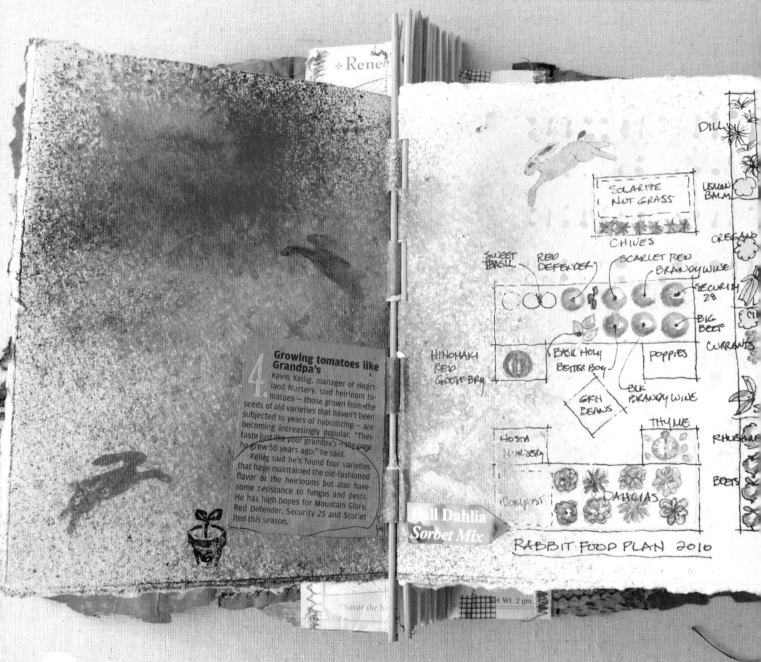

fig. C

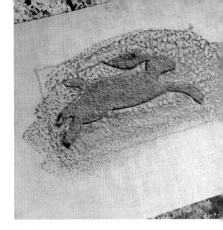

fig. D

WHAT YOU'LL NEED

* Paper
* Spray bottle with water
* Water-based dye or diluted acrylic paint in a spray bottle
* Texture stamp
* Inkpad
* Craft foam (optional)
* Adhesive fabric sheet
* Sharp craft knife
* Teardrop-shaped pigment inkpad
* Craft glue
* Watercolors
* Colored pencils
* Fine-point black marker

TECHNIQUE

1   Spray a single light spritz of water on the paper and follow up with a spritz of water-based dye before the water dries. To spread the color around spray additional water as desired. Let the page dry **(fig. A)**.

2   Stamp textures onto the page.

3   Scan an image of a rabbit or other figure and print it onto an adhesive fabric sheet that has a peel-off backing. (Adhesive fabric sheets are available at quilt shops, craft stores, and online stores.) Cut out a generous allowance around the printed figure. Then cut out the figure very carefully with a sharp craft knife. Remember that you'll be using the leftover area as a stencil **(fig. B)**.

4   Peel the backing off the cut-out figure and put the backing aside. Adhere the fabric figure to the journal page.

5   Place the figure backing on a separate work surface. If the image is very small, like mine, stick it down with removable double-faced tape. Ink over it with a hand-held teardrop-shaped pigment inkpad and allow it to dry.

6   Remove the backing image. Glue it onto the journal page **(fig. C)**.

7   As mentioned in step 3, use the fabric left over from the cutout to stencil the figure on the page with a stamp pad. For reversed figures (facing in the opposite direction), flip the stencil over and ink it from the other side **(fig. D)**.

8   Add small garden illustrations with watercolors and colored pencils.

9   Add journaling with a black fine-point marker.

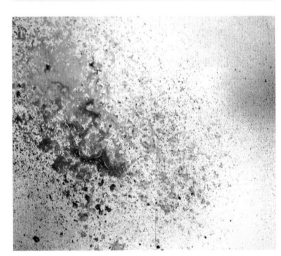

fig. A

fig. B

Front Door Planters

For the right-hand page, I made a color toner-based copy of a plant tag and transferred the image onto paper (see Citra Solv Transfers on opposite page). I placed a second transfer on the back side of the page, then stitched the edges together, front to back. This allowed both sides of the page to look great.

On the front side, I made a slit for a pocket, then inserted and adhered other elements. I decorated the pocket with a strip of ribbon threaded through a piece of plant tag, punched with a threading punch. I stamped a page stamp at the bottom and a rectangular label stamp on the side, then added watercolors. I painted a picture of the planter with the plants in it, adding a few printed notes.

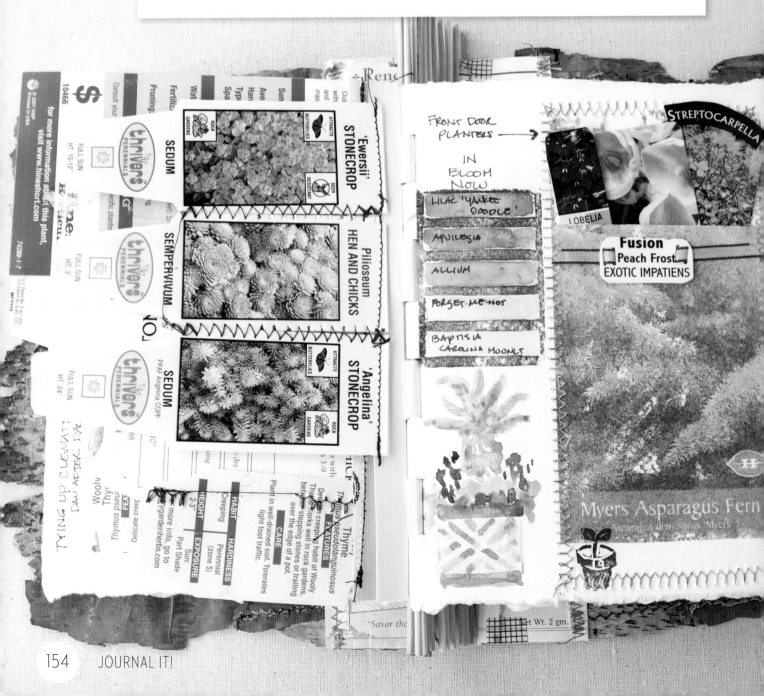

INSIGHT

Amazingly, this is one page where everything worked as planned the first time around. I especially like the way the transfers worked, yielding a sort of fuzzy, worn look to the page.

CITRA SOLV TRANSFERS

Citra Solv is a natural citrus cleaner and degreaser that many artists and crafters use to transfer images onto paper and fabric. You need to make a toner-based copy of an image that you'd like to transfer. Inkjet printer copies do not work for this method, so take your image to a copy center. Place the toner-based copy onto the paper, image side down. Paint the back side of the paper with Citra Solv. Burnish the image with the bottom of a spoon. Peel off the paper to reveal the transferred image.

About the Contributors

JULIE FEI-FAN BALZER is a self-taught mixed-media collage artist and avid scrapbooker whose work can be seen in numerous publications and on several TV shows. She lives in New York City with her husband. To learn more visit *balzerdesigns.typepad.com.*

JILL K. BERRY is a graphic designer and painter living in Superior, Colorado with her husband and two kids. Her work can be seen in numerous publications. To learn more about her visit *jillberrydesign.com.*

SARAH ATWATER BOURNE is a Philadelphia-based artist who is currently pursuing a master's of fine arts in book arts and printmaking from The University of the Arts. To learn more about her visit *sarahatwaterbourne.com.*

ALISA BURKE is a painter and mixed-media artist living in San Diego, California. When she's not making art, she's traveling the country teaching workshops. For more information visit *alisaburke.com.*

DEBRA COOPER is a mixed-media artist, designer, and home-schooling mom of two. She lives in Pueblo, Colorado. To see more of Debra's work or to learn more about her visit *debracooperart.com.*

BELINDA FIREMAN is an artist and mother of twin girls and a boy. She lives in Calgary, Alberta, Canada, where she paints in mostly acrylic and watercolors. Learn more about Belinda at *belindafireman.com.*

BOB FISHER is an Atlanta-based artist, designer, and writer who turned to sketchbooks to inspire creativity and keep his sanity. Bob shares his sketchbooks and thoughts about creativity at *sketchbob.com.*

SUSANNA GORDON is a Canadian living in the United States. She studied art and photography at the Ontario College of Art & Design in Toronto. To see more of her artwork, visit *susannassketchbook. typepad.com.*

BRUCE KREMER has filled dozens of sketchbooks and diaries over the past thirty years, many of which have been featured in exhibits across the country as well as in books. He lives in Ketchum, Idaho. To learn more visit *bkremer.com.*

KATHRIN JEBSEN-MARWEDEL is a photographer and designer living in Kiel, Germany. To learn more about her and see more of her work visit *flickr.com/ photos/98657307@N00/.*

COREY MOORTGAT is a Florida-based collage artist, stay-at-home mother, wife, sewer, and thrift shopper. She has been published in numerous publications as well as in her own book, The Art of Personal Imagery. To learn more about her, visit *coreymoortgat.blogspot.com.*

MELANIE MOWINSKI is an Assistant Professor of Visual Art at the Massachusetts College of Liberal Arts in North Adams, Massachusetts. Her work can be seen in numerous private and public collections. To learn more about her, visit *melaniemowinski.com.*

ZOM OSBORNE is an Australia-based artist. Her work has been seen in numerous exhibitions. To learn more about her visit *pinchmetoseeifyouaredreaming. blogspot.com.*

JEANETTE SCLAR is a Kansas City-based artist who is particularly inspired by nature, especially her garden patch filled with rabbits. To learn more about her vis *despatchesfromlongears.blogspot.com.*

CAROLYN SEWELL is a Washington, D.C.-based artist who decided she wanted to be a graphic designer in the eighth grade. When she's not designing for clients, she works on her postcard projects. You can learn more about those as well as her other artwork, at *carolynsewell.com.*

SUSAN SHELLEY believes there are no rules in art, and instead chooses to focus on how best she can accomplish whatever she wants to on any given day in her journal. Journaling has enriched her life by tying memories from the past together with current events.

ROBEN-MARIE SMITH is a mixed-media collage artist living in Port Orange, Florida. She is the owner and designer of Paperbag Studios, which offers a full line of rubber stamps. To learn more about her, visit *robenmarie.com.*

ANNA-MARIA WOLNIAK is a painter and photographer living in Poland. She has a passion for scrapbooking, especially when the subject is her son. To see more of her artwork, visit *annamariawolniak. wordpress.com.*

ALISON WORMAN is a student at the Maryland Institute College of Art, where she's majoring in fibers and concentrating in book arts. To learn more about her and see more of her artwork visit *alisonworman.com.*

Resources

GLOSSARY OF TERMS

acrylic paint Fast-drying water-based paint, with results that can resemble a watercolor or oil painting. When dry, the paint is opaque.

adhesive fabric sheet Fabric sheets that can be run through a color inkjet printer. The backing can be peeled off and the image applied to other surfaces. Commonly used in quilting.

bone folder A craft tool used to make creases in paper; it can be made of actual bone or from plastic.

calligraphy The art of fine hand lettering, usually with a special pen and nib (the point of the pen).

china marker Also known as a grease pencil, this wax writing tool was designed for writing on glass, plastic, and other polished surfaces. The outer casing may be made of wood and sharpened like an ordinary pencil, or covered in paper and sharpened by pulling a string.

chisel-tip marker A style of felt-tipped marker that has an angled point, with a marking capability that resembles a calligraphy pen.

collage An art form in which a variety of papers, fabric, photos, and/or other relatively flat items are arranged and glued on paper.

colorless blender A colored pencil that contains wax and fillers but no pigment, used to blend and soften the edges of colored pencil artwork; or a felt-tipped marker that works in the same way with color markers.

Coptic binding A bookbinding method developed by early Christians know as Copts; the process involves stitching through the folded edges of paper to hold them together.

craft foam A thin, flexible foam sheet used for shaping various crafts and costumes; A sheet of craft foam can be used as backing behind a journal page to prevent bleed-through of ink.

craft knife This metal knife, also called a utility knife, has a razor-sharp blade that can be replaced when dull. When using a craft knife to cut papers, use a metal ruler and be very careful where you put your fingers.

decoupage glue A kind of glue used to secure layers of paper; can be painted on the top of the papers and will dry clear.

detail scissors Primarily used for sewing, especially embroidery, these small scissors have very fine, sharp points for cutting in tight areas.

ephemera In art, ephemera refers to collectible bits of paper from daily life, such as greeting cards, letters, posters, tickets, wrappers, and other scraps.

gel medium A clear acrylic substance with the thickness of hair gel, used to change the consistency of acrylic paint; in journaling, this medium is used for image transfer (page 139).

gel pen A pen with water-based ink that tends to be thick and opaque, resulting in rich pigments on the page.

gesso This white paint mixture is used to prepare/prime surfaces for painting. In journaling, gesso can be used to paint over colored surfaces for a muting or mottling effect.

giclée A fine art digital print made on ink-jet printers.

gouache A form of watercolor paint that is opaque rather than transparent.

graphite stick Graphite (the same material that is in pencils) in a large, chunky form, similar to pastel sticks or jumbo crayons.

inks Ink comes in many colors, forms, and thicknesses; it can be permanent or water-soluble. Ink can be applied with an airbrush, pen, or a brush; ink sprays are also available.

marking crayon Similar to a china marker, this wax marker can write on a variety of surfaces.

monoprinting Printmaking methods are generally used to print an image many times, but a monoprint is only printed once. Paint, collage, or other mediums are often added to make the print unique.

nib The tip of a pen; the part that releases ink onto a page. Many types, sizes, and shapes are available.

palette A board, glass, plastic sheet, or container designed to hold a range of artist colors (usually paint). The word "palette" can also refer to the range of colors used in a particular painting.

palette knife A small tool with a flexible steel blade used for mixing or applying paint.

palimpsest A manuscript that has been written on more than once, with the earlier writing incompletely erased and still partially visible on the page.

papier-mâché A form of arts and crafts that involves layering and pasting many strips of paper, which hardens into a shape; typically used in mask-making.

pastels An art medium of powdered pigment that has been compressed into a stick pencil, or crayon for drawing.

PVA (polyvinyl acetate) glue White glue, widely available, which dries clear. Higher-quality pH neutral versions are used in bookbinding.

quill pen An early writing implement with a nib made from the feather of a large bird.

stencil A thin sheet of material, such as paper, plastic, or metal, with letters or a design cut from it; when the stencil is placed on a surface and painted, the cutout shape will appear on the surface. Typically a stencil is used to spell out words or repeat a shape in a design.

sticky sheets Adhesive sheets, designed for scrapbooking and other paper crafts, that work like double-sided tape. Sheets can be cut into shapes, peeled, and applied to paper in a variety of ways.

substrate Primary or underlying material on which other materials, such as ink, paper, paint, or other layers, are applied.

walnut ink Literally, ink made from the husk of a walnut. Often used to stain and darken paper to make it look older.

watercolor paint Paint made with pigments suspended in a water-soluble medium; when dry, the colors are transparent.

water-soluble crayons Crayons that can be used for drawing, then brushed with water for a watercolor effect.

wonky In art, wonky means deliberately askew or off-center.

ART PRODUCTS

When it comes to choosing your supplies, the range of options can be overwhelming. Don't let that stop you! If you don't see something that suits you at a local craft store or art supply store, do some research online until you find the right fit. Below are some products to get you started; most can be found at one or more of the art suppliers listed. Additional sources may be listed with individual products.

ART SUPPLIERS ONLINE

www.artrsupplywarehouse.com
www.danielsmith.com
www.dickblick.com
www.cheapjoes.com
www.jacquardproducts.com
www.jerrysartarama.com
www.michaels.com
www.utrechtart.com

ADHESIVES
Lineco Neutral pH Adhesive
Bookbinder-quality, white PVA glue.

Mod Podge
A milky white liquid glue that dries transparent, advertised as an all-in-one glue, sealer, and finish. Used for decoupage and for other paper and mixed-media projects.

Inks
Brilliance Archival Inkpads
Teardrop-shaped inkpads that can be used for stamping or applied directly to paper.

Glimmer Mist Tints
Created for scrapbooking; water-based, acid-free, nontoxic color in a spray bottle. mytatteredangels.com

Tim Holtz Adirondack Color Wash
Acid-free, nontoxic, water-based ink that can be used on paper, fibers, and fabrics. www.rangerink.com/products

JOURNALS, SKETCHBOOKS, AND PAPERS
Arches Watercolor Paper
Produced in France for over 500 years; cold-pressed, acid-free, 100-percent cotton paper available in different weights, and in single sheets, blocks, or field sketchbooks.

American Journey Artist Sketchbook
Hard-backed, spiral-bound sketchbook with 70-lb paper. www.cheapjoes.com

American Masters Printmaking Paper
Acid-free paper made from 100-percent cotton rag; originally developed as a printmaking paper, but also suitable for drawing and watercolors. www.utrechtart.com

Canson Basic and Field Sketchbooks
Hardcover sketchbooks with spiral binding and acid-free 65-lb paper.

Global Art Handbook Journals
Hardcover sketchbook with heavyweight, acid-free drawing paper and elastic closure.

Moleskine
Well-respected maker of softcover and hardcover lined journals and unlined watercolor sketchbooks, with acid-free paper and elastic closure. www.moleskine.com

Rives Printmaking Paper
Made in France; acid-free, 100-percent cotton paper developed for printmaking, but also suitable for other art forms.

Strathmore Paper
Fine art paper produced in a variety of weights and sizes, available in sheets and pads.
www.strathmoreartist.com

MARKERS, PENS, AND PENCILS

Brause
Specializes in calligraphy pens and nibs.
www.brause-kalligraphie.com

Caran d'Ache
Maker of high-quality ink pens, water-soluble crayons, water-soluble fiber-tipped pens, and watercolor pencils.

Copic
Maker of high-quality markers that are available in over 300 colors; some styles are refillable. They also make Multiliner pens, with or without refillable ink cartridges, and replaceable nibs. Disposable fountain pens are also available.
www.copicmarker.com

Cynscribe Calligraphy Directory
Resource for calligraphers and bookmakers; lists suppliers, conferences, exhibitions, and events, among other things.
www.cynscribe.com

Eberhard Faber
Manufacturer of many art products, including colored pencils, wax crayons, watercolor pencils, pastels, and gel pens.
www.eberhardfaber.com

Faber-Castell
Makes a variety of drawing products, including Pitt calligraphy pens, pastel pencils, Polychromos colored pencil sets, watercolor pencils, and brush-tip pens.

FabricMate
These brush-tip pens contain permanent dye that is blendable, available in fine art colors; available in chisel-tip.

Holbein
Maker of numerous art mediums, including acrylics, gouache, drawing inks, water-based oils, oils, pastels, watercolors, and water-soluble crayons.
www.holbeinhk.com

Horizon
Top-of-the line brass calligraphy pens.

JetPens
Japanese supplier of a wide range of fountain pens, gel pens, brush pens, calligraphy pens, highlighters, and more.
www.jetpens.com

Koh-I-Noor Rapidograph
High-quality technical pens that have been on the market for over 30 years. Precise, consistent lines; a wide range of point sizes; commonly available in sets.

Pentel
Makes hybrid gel-ink pens; ink is permanent and fade-proof; some fluorescent colors available. Also makes the Aquash water brush; use this watercolor crayons to spread and smooth colors.

Pilot Latte
Gel-ink pens available in a pastel color series.

Prismacolor
Offers a wide variety of professional art and drawing supplies, including colored pencil sets, sketch and charcoal pencils, art markers, and watercolor pencils.
www.prismacolor.com

Sakura Pigma Micron Pens
Disposable technical pen with archival pigmented ink; range of colors and nib sizes for a variety of line widths.

Sharpie
Maker primarily of marker pens, including oil-based fine-point silver paint markers.

Stabilo Aquarellable
Waterproof wax marking pencils designed to mark on a glass, vinyl, and polished surfaces; available in limited colors.

Staedtler
This German company is known for fine writing instruments and technical pens; produces a wide range of writing products, including fine-point color markers.

Staonal
General marking crayons, wax-based; permanent and waterproof.

Uni-ball
Maker of Signo gel pens and micro deluxe (rollerball, waterproof) pens.

PAINTING SUPPLIES

Liquitex
Offers a wide spectrum of acrylic paints, mediums, and art supplies, including gel medium that can be used in image transfer.
www.liquitex.com

Golden Artist Colors
Maker of professional grade acrylic paint and mediums, including gel medium that can be used in image transfer.
www.goldenpaints.com

Index

About the Author

Jenny Doh is founder of *www.crescendoh.com* and lover of art. She is author of numerous books including *We Make Dolls*, *Hand in Hand*, and *Signature Styles*. She lives in Santa Ana, California, with her husband and two children.